'A welcome addition to the discourse on how boards
roles and responsibilities to meet the governance
relentless competitive disruption, unprecedented technological upheaval, and amorphous geopolitics.'

Rama Bijapurkar,
prominent Independent Director from India

'This is a splendid book; it offers profound and wise insights into how boards need to think, behave and act if they are to be truly effective, derived from an impressive lifetime's journey which has given Shefaly the extraordinary richness and breadth of experience on which to draw in offering them, which she does with a combination of clarity of thought, bluntness in addressing the issues which are so often evaded, and honest intelligence about the informal aspects of creating a great decision-making environment.

This breadth of perspective – cultural and geographical – shines through in every part of the book, and it is central to her thinking about how boards can best navigate decision-making in an era of rising complexity and unpredictability: diversity and difference – of background, thought, style – are not optional extras or boxes to be ticked: they are absolutely core to the delivery of better performance by boards.'

Sir Ivan Rogers,
KCMG

'As an experienced Executive Board Director – and a recently engaged Non-Executive Director – I feel Shefaly Yogendra's book comes at a very timely moment. You will find this work inspiring, stretching and wholly relevant to the challenges faced by Board members today. At a time of "disposable life" colliding with the "stratospheric growth" of AI, more than ever, Board members must come with a mind-set attuned to volatility, uncertainty, incomprehension, and... future readiness. Simply, this book will make you think and make you stretch. A most highly recommended partner to accompany your Board journey.'

Adam J. Middleton,
global energy sector executive, adviser, non-executive board director, and Chair

'This book is a bold and timely reimagining of what true board leadership means in an era demanding agility, vision, and accountability. With clarity and conviction, it challenges traditional boardroom orthodoxy and ushers in a new paradigm of adaptive, forward-looking leadership.'

Joanna Bonnett,
Non-executive director, Riverside Finance Ltd and former board member and President of the Association of Corporate Treasurers

'My work spans continents, sectors, and disciplines, so I recognize immediately when someone understands that governance isn't one-size-fits-all. Shefaly Yogendra gets it. She writes about what boards actually need in volatile environments: strategic stamina, not compliance theatre. Foresight, not hindsight dressed up as oversight. The ability to govern technology while still learning about it. Her focus on boardroom dynamics and psychological safety reflects what I see working with organizations navigating complexity across markets; the human elements determine whether strategic thinking actually happens or gets performative. This is governance writing grounded in the reality boards actually face.'

Tiffany A. Archer, Esq.,
attorney, academic, Founder & President of Eunomia Risk Advisory, Co-Chair of the New York City Bar Association's Task Force on Behavioral Science & Digital Technologies, inaugural member of the Wall Street Journal Board of Directors Council

'*Uncharted Spaces* is the ultimate handbook every working professional whether a founder or first-time director should have within reach. Most books on boards and business are written from the top down. This one is written from the trenches; the messy, high-velocity world where most businesses actually operate. Drawing on lived experience, Dr Shefaly weaves in everything from unpacking the relationship between the Chair and the CEO, to showing how geopolitics influences decision-making, to explaining "when" the board actually steps in. This book doesn't miss a beat.

As the world moves towards inclusive innovation and as cultural IP frameworks strengthen across the globe, this book reinforces that future-focused boards and board leadership demand both awareness and agility. They must think deeply about (their) social licence to operate and responsible stewardship. Whether it's Kohlapuris, Labubus or coffee, nations with rich heritage will defend what's theirs with equal voice, potentially turning what may seem like short-term business opportunities into long-term liabilities.

Spanning lessons from Guyana to Ghana and the UK to India, *Uncharted Spaces* is for anyone curious, transitioning to or already at the boardroom table, it's one of the most practical and globally aware 101s on modern board rooms.'

Eshna Gogia,
ecosystem builder, founder of DeepTechFest Ireland, Top 100 people in Irish Tech (2024, 2025)

'Being a woman on a board in Southeast Asia is like being a yak in heels on the bridge of a ship in a massive typhoon, and there weren't any books that provided any wisdom before this one.

Navigating the thicket of compliance and keeping an organization loyal to its evolving vision is a challenge for any professional. Shefaly provides a compass for those of us who seek to profit with a purpose and engage younger generations to keep their fingers out but their noses in everything, as new board members.'

Maoi Arroyo,
multi-award-winning entrepreneur, impact investor, educator, Entrepreneur magazine's 35-under-35 (2006), DevEx 40-under-40 International Development Leaders (2013), UK Foreign Commonwealth Office's International Leaders (2014), World Economic Forum Young Global Leader (2015), member, Global Future Council on investing to achieve the UN Sustainable Development Goals (2020–2022)

'In this fierce and deeply intelligent reframing of modern governance. Shefaly Yogendra gives language to the experiences many of us have lived but never articulated. A masterclass in modern stewardship, this book is a gift to anyone stepping into board leadership. I wish I had read this at the start of my board journey!'

Arushi Chopra,
global sustainability strategist and adviser to leaders navigating complex transitions to build strategic advantage

'The book reads as a curious literary illusion – at once a series of concepts illustrated in an almost case study format while weaving a tapestry of such incredibly human stories to immerse the reader in boardrooms across the globe. A recommended read for anyone seeking ideas for a more resilient future – ideas born from extensive research and years of reflective experience.'

Pranav Sridhar,
impact led growth leader in Africa and Asia, co-founder and board director of One Day Health in Uganda

'As a younger person, with endless curiosity and a complexity science brain, my favourite idea in the book was that boards require thinkers of complexity but communicators of simplicity. And that simplicity did not equal specialised isolation, but a temperament of seeking cohesion across differences of ideas and opinions.

My generation is a little weary of complicated, cryptic, and normative statements so I found the honesty and simple truths in the book appealing, and quite absorbable.

This book felt to me like a pocket dictionary of experience and applied systems thinking, a guide which actually doesn't feel impossible to apply. Even beyond boardrooms, I feel it can help navigate the ever-changing possibilities around us.'

Samuel S. Harris,
historian, multidisciplinary problem-solver, young stakeholder in the future being shaped in boardrooms

Shefaly M. Yogendra, PhD

Reset
the agenda.

Reimagine
the boardroom.

First published in Great Britain by Practical Inspiration Publishing, 2026

ISBN 9781788608770 (paperback)
9781788608763 (hardback)
9781788608787 (ebook)

EU GPSR representative: LOGOS EUROPE, 9 rue Nicolas Poussin, LA ROCHELLE 17000, France Contact@logoseurope.eu

Contents

Foreword

By Fiona Hathorn

Co-Founder and CEO of WB Directors, formerly Women on Boards UK, a purpose-led business working to increase diversity in executive and non-executive leadership. WB Directors has just joined forces with Nurole, a specialist board search and advisory firm helping organizations hire, develop, and evaluate non-executive leaders to build future-fit boards.

***

When Shefaly Yogendra joined the Women on Boards UK network, we knew she brought a distinct voice to the conversation around modern governance. What we didn't know – but quickly came to recognize – was just how deeply she would challenge, provoke, and expand what many of us thought was possible in the boardroom.

Shefaly's book, *Uncharted Spaces: Reset the Agenda. Reimagine the Boardroom*, is a timely, urgent, and intelligent invitation to reconsider what boardrooms are for – and who belongs in them. Unlike so many who follow a well-worn corporate path to board service, Shefaly has crafted her own. Entrepreneur, academic, governance professional, and relentless truth-teller – she brings a rare combination of intellectual rigour, commercial acumen, and personal courage.

Her insights are drawn not just from years of experience on listed boards, investment trusts, and public institutions, but also from a deep commitment to governance that works for the future – not just for the status quo. She has chaired remuneration, nomination, governance, ESG, and audit & risk committees with a cool head and a sharp mind, and mentored CEOs and directors with equal parts insight and candour. Her PhD in decision-making isn't just a credential – it underpins her thinking on how boards can, and must, make better decisions in an increasingly complex world.

This book is not a manual – it is a manifesto. Through personal narrative, practical advice, and reflections from others who have navigated both conventional and unconventional paths to the boardroom, Shefaly constructs a blueprint for resilience, relevance, and responsibility. She doesn't tell us what to think; she teaches us how to think more clearly, act more boldly, and engage more ethically.

Shefaly's perspective is unflinching. Her writing – much like her boardroom presence – is direct, incisive, and unapologetically smart. She brings with her not only the credibility of lived experience but also a deep sense of integrity and duty to good governance. She does not perform difference; she embodies it. She reminds us that representation without rigour is meaningless. It is not enough to 'have a seat at the table' – one must know how to use it, and when necessary, build a new table entirely.

In this book, Shefaly lifts the lid on what really happens in boardrooms. She dares to speak truths that many gloss over: about toxic cultures, performative governance, and the uncomfortable silences that hinder challenge. She understands that diversity – of thought, background, and approach – is only valuable when paired with inclusion and psychological safety. And she shows us how to cultivate both.

Shefaly also reminds us – without apology – that difference matters. Not just for its own sake, but for the commercial, cultural, and ethical strength it brings to decision-making. As she has often said, 'Complex problems of the future will not be solved by applying narrow functional and disciplinary training and tools of the past'. Her lived example – and this book – demonstrate exactly how we might begin to reimagine the boardroom: not as a room of the usual suspects, but as a space where courage, curiosity, and competence meet.

The structure of *Uncharted Spaces* is itself a reflection of Shefaly's clarity of thinking. The first part charts her journey – non-linear, deeply thoughtful, and highly intentional. It's a generous offering to those who want to learn how to build a board career differently, on their own terms. The second part is a masterclass in boardroom dynamics, drawing on real stories and offering practical wisdom. The final sections offer a compelling look ahead – a provocation for where governance must go if it is to remain relevant in a world defined by geopolitical flux, technological disruption, and environmental urgency.

I have had the privilege of seeing Shefaly's journey unfold – not as a straight line, but as a considered and principled evolution. Her success is not an accident; it is the result of intention, reflection, and sheer determination. For every reader – aspiring or seasoned director – this book is a companion and a challenge. It asks you not just to find your place in the boardroom, but to help reshape it.

And perhaps most powerfully, Shefaly shows us that it is possible to lead without conforming. To contribute meaningfully without mimicking. To be an outsider – and still create change from within. In doing so, she offers a path not just to others who feel different, but to organizations seeking truly effective governance in a fast-changing world.

If you are serious about the future of governance, about making boards better, braver, and more inclusive, then this is the book you need. And Shefaly Yogendra is the guide you want.

Fiona Hathorn,
Founder-CEO WB Directors

Preface

2015 was a year of reflection. Livyora, the luxury tech venture I built for three years with two co-founders, had to be wound up. My father, with whom I had had a deeply affectionate, comforting, chatty, and enjoyable relationship since my childhood, experienced a femoral fracture which severely curtailed his freedom, quality of life, and ultimately lifespan. In pondering the professional and the personal, I tuned into myself.

My career began in India in the mid-1990s in corporate venturing – a fancy term for creating new business units, launching new brands and product categories, working in functions as disparate as logistics and product marketing, and opening new markets.

This meant that even as a freshly baked management graduate, and despite the creative chaos in those jobs, I came to see business as a connected whole, instead of as a sum of disjointed, specialized functional parts. Working in business in such capacities also brought alive what had been abstract ideas in my university education in engineering: systems thinking and feedback loops. I further realized that a business as a system had particular qualities – those intrinsic to it, and those shaped by its functioning in an external environment often outside its spheres of control and influence. And above all, I came to see how leaders had the power and indeed the responsibility to shape business in meaningful and financially sustainable ways.

In England, as an immigrant, I found myself building a portfolio career, a futuristic term coined by the late Professor Charles Handy in 1989.

Having been an intrapreneur, an entrepreneur, a manager, an adviser, and an adjunct professor, by 2015 I had grown into a business generalist with a nerdy mainline in emerging technologies and their impact on shaping societal and organizational culture. I had also had the opportunity to live in dozens of cities on three continents, speaking several languages and eavesdropping in several more. Well-regarded academic institutions in India, the UK, and the USA had provided me intellectual homes and shaped the conceptual foundations of my ability to bring first-principles thinking to complex, emergent matters.

My curiosity had remained undimmed; my education in engineering and management, followed by a second stint studying policy and decision-making, had given me an unusual toolkit to frame and solve problems; my advisory experience meant I retained my independence and was not embedded in any one industry or company or network, building bridges across things that rarely come together.

Conversations with fellow professionals in 2015 made me appreciate afresh the value of the uncommon *Weltanschauung* shaped by my formative and lived experiences. My independence of mind, good judgement, stomach for uncertainty, ability to build sustainable structures in creative chaos, and calmness under duress were all qualities boardrooms would appreciate and value, I was advised. I took that advice on board.

Come January 2016, I started a Board Apprenticeship with JP Morgan US Smaller Companies Investment Trust, hosted and supported by an incredible chairman[1] and a strong board. This became the launchpad into my journey as an independent board director.

Fast forward to the summer of 2024, and a friend who has had a stellar executive career in a tough, male-dominated industry rang me: 'If you were starting now on your board director journey, Shefaly, how would you go about it?' she asked.

> I had no pat answer for her. For things had changed since 2016, when I began.

The job of governance is much harder now, with a vortex of change engulfing us. Stewardship is urgently needed as we are accountable to the future generations for whom we seek to preserve and grow wealth, while protecting this planet.

As the wisdom goes, *plus ça change, plus c'est la même chose*, and some things have not changed at all. There is cynicism about boards and what they do. Board positions are seen as entitled, nepotistic jobs-for-the-boys, and easy-going retirement gigs where everyone agrees with everyone, collects fees, wines and dines at the company's expense, and goes home or to the golf course.

The reality is liminal. Boards are transitioning from that caricature to something the shape of which cannot yet be predicted firmly, but is slowly emerging. Amid the cognizance of the complexity of challenges and changes is also growing acknowledgement that those challenges require different governance structures and conversations, very different people around the table, and frequent reviews of any functioning board's own continuing relevance.

The emergent space will look quite different in the next three to five years. The change is subtle but in evidence.

This book is therefore about more than just my story. It is about many directors' journeys to the boardroom, boardroom conversations around the world, urgent considerations of technology, climate change and geopolitics, and how these considerations are catalysing the reimagining of boardrooms that reset their agenda to remain relevant for the future being shaped in front of our eyes.

1

How it started…

I took my first board role in my mid-20s, in Switzerland, perhaps unfashionably early. I joined my first listed board in my early 40s, perhaps unfashionably early for many traditional careerists. I am not a traditional careerist though I did begin that way.

My story is not the centre of this book but it does belong somewhere on the spectrum of people getting started serving on boards and people rotating off boards into the sunset. I hope this book will help you locate your own story and journey on that spectrum.

My story

Know thyself!

I recently reorganized my library. It is an overwhelming undertaking and a comforting revelation to see one's own arc of growth through the books on one's bookcases.

The golden thread throughout? Curiosity.

As a curious and observant child, I loved watching my polymathic older cousin do things during one of his visits to see us: he replaced a worn-out tuner string and a valve in our mid-20th century radio, showing me how it tuned into the frequency for BBC World Service; he then changed the needle on the record-player, explaining to me why vinyl records had grooves on them; after that he unpicked the stitching on his bell-bottom trousers, and cut and sewed them into the new shape that was the emerging fashion; and finally he cooked a mean goat curry for dinner, pulling together a delicate balance of spices and cuts of meat.

Problems, I learnt early, were solvable if we took the time to understand the various moving and static parts, their role in relation to other moving and static parts, and their function as a whole.

Turns out there is a second golden thread here. Patience.

These two pillars were how, when unable to find willing employers as a new immigrant in the UK, I shrugged and persisted in building a 'portfolio career'. I worked with a range of stakeholders – regulators, legislators, investors, business leaders, founders and creators, civil society groups – and developed an empathetic and deep understanding of how they fitted together as moving or static parts in the broad environment in which societies functioned and gave businesses the social licence to operate.

Engineering taught me how to define a problem fulsomely, management studies taught me about resource allocation, and policy studies helped me understand power politics and agendas. I had the right first-principles toolkit to deconstruct nearly every problem that came my way.

My curiosity and patience meant I had read extensively across disciplines – hence those creaking bookcases – and thinking like an engineer, built a contextual map of the world and geopolitical dynamics. My early adoption of social platforms meant I had honed the skill to pick up on small signals and crowd sentiment, and developed solid strategic foresight for surfacing both risk and opportunity.

Who could make use of all my training, experience, and knowledge without forcing me into a narrow functional box?

Enter the boardroom![1]

In 2015, when I wanted to change the direction of my career, I was not only seeking a context where my capabilities would be of service, but also trying to balance my work with my caregiving responsibilities that were unpredictable and needed flexibility. The work of an independent director on boards of companies sounded like the right opportunity.

This was my 'why'.

The 'why' is important; it comes before 'how'.

How it unfolded

Conversations with a range of friends and clients, and the serendipitous discovery of the Board Apprentice programme got me started. The rest that followed is why this book is in your hands right now. My hope is that my unusual journey – and the journeys of others whose stories you will find in the following pages – will help answer my friend's question: 'If you were starting now on your board director journey, Shefaly, how would you go about it?'

Soon after starting the board apprenticeship in 2016, I joined WB Directors (then called Women on Boards UK), a purpose-led business and the UK's leading board directors' community. My first board appointment was a trusteeship with Beyond Me, a millennial-founded charity aiming to enable millennial philanthropy. I found the role advertised on WB Directors and applied just before the deadline. There were shortlisting and interview rounds, and I was appointed to the trustee board.

In the autumn of 2016, almost three-quarters of the way through my board apprenticeship, the board of JP Morgan US Smaller Companies Investment Trust (stock symbol: JUSC) wanted to recruit a new director in the course of succession planning and asked me if I was interested in joining the board. I had by this time met with the portfolio management team in New York during the board's annual trip. My apprenticeship being at no cost to shareholders, I had chosen to pay my way for the travel but I was included in the meetings, and the board dinner with the portfolio management team. This had given them a chance to meet me and see my style of engagement, scrutiny, and seeking understanding. I was thrilled to be asked and joined the board, without even completing my 12 months as an apprentice.

In late 2016, I was invited to speak on a panel for the launch of a Policy Exchange report on glass ceilings faced by ethnic minorities in business and other professions.[2] I was 'talent-spotted' in the room and subsequently approached by the headhunter helping London Metropolitan University with their board recruitment at the time. Following an interview process, I joined the University's board in May 2017. During an eventful and energizing six-year term, I served as Interim Chair, Vice Chair, Chair of audit & risk and of governance committees, member of the remuneration committee as well as panel chair and member for hiring a Vice Chancellor (University CEO), a deputy Vice Chancellor, and several board directors.

In 2018, following the death of my father, I took on a full-time role as the Chief Operating Officer of a symbolic AI company, and became an executive director on the board. This role came via a timely introduction to the IP Group, who were the Series A investor in the company and were looking for a commercial, senior executive to serve alongside the two founders on the executive team. I was encouraged by the Chair to keep my external boards, as I was the only board-experienced executive on the team and he was keen to establish sustainable governance and accountability mechanisms in the company.

In 2019 I was approached by a headhunter who was conducting a search for a FTSE 250 board that had – and continues to have – intellectual heft drawn from cognitive diversity. I met the board for a conversation. We had a rolling discussion around the table on a range of topics including exclusion or engagement, macroeconomics, the future of investment companies, and so on. That was how I was appointed to the Temple Bar Investment Trust (stock symbol: TMPL) board, whereas of 2025 I serve as the Senior Independent Director, chair the nomination committee, and also serve on the informal marketing committee, having chaired the management engagement committee earlier.

In the summer of 2021, I was approached to consider joining a board that was about to do an IPO (Initial Public Offering) to raise funding for a grid-scale battery storage company with 2h-duration assets in the UK.[3] I did not know any of the other proposed directors. Following a long chat with the putative Chair, who rode his motorbike to come and meet me where I live, and several due diligence conversations including with the proposed asset management team, I agreed to join the board. We worked all summer in preparation for the IPO. In November 2021, we took Harmony Energy Income Trust (stock symbol: HEIT) to listing on the main market on the London Stock Exchange, in the Specialist Funds segment and as a Green Economy company. In June 2025, the company was acquired and subsequently delisted from the London Stock Exchange.

Autumn 2021 saw an approach from the Royal Academy of Engineering, where I was known to several people due to my work with iTeams in Cambridge during my student days, my having given a talk to the MPhil in technology policy cohort 18 years prior to the approach, and my having spoken on panels alongside their CEO on a couple of occasions. The Academy is one of the UK's learned societies and it was a privilege to be invited to join the Enterprise Committee, where I still serve. As of 2025 I also serve on the Fundraising Committee and the judging panel for the prestigious Bhattacharyya Award that celebrates sustained, strategic industry-academia collaboration. I contribute to panels as Chair and speaker, mentor founders on the Shott accelerator, and support many of our fellowship and awards programmes.

In late 2022, I was approached by another headhunter conducting a search for a FTSE 250 board. Following interviews, I was invited to join the board of Witan Investment Trust (stock symbol: WTAN) and Witan Investment Services in 2023. I served on the marketing committee of the latter board and was added to the Financial Conduct Authority's SM&CR (Senior Managers and Certification Regime) register thanks to the company supporting the process. Following the merger with Alliance Trust in 2024, I came off the Witan board.

In January 2025, I joined, as an independent director, the board of Ampa LLP which is the world's largest B-Corp in legal services. The 'House of Brands™' is pursuing strategic growth and technological transformation and I look forward to contributing to both.

During this time, I have remained an active participant and contributor in several directors' communities (see **Resources** towards the end of the book). I help aspiring board directors with their CVs and help them prepare for their interviews. I also advise directors privately when they find themselves in challenging situations on their boards. I continue to conduct board training sessions mostly on emerging topics in technology and geopolitics, and also coach board-adjacent CXOs on being more effective and successful in their work.

When a headhunter rings me for candidate referrals or soft references or indeed formal references, I channel my inner Tom Cruise ('Help me help you!') and refer people to roles, and provide well-substantiated references. On occasion I have advised smaller headhunting firms to rethink their marketing so as to improve their brand recall and consideration when boards are working on succession. In the last few years, I have found myself being cited in headhunter reports on board-relevant topics, invited to attend exclusive events, and asked to share my expertise especially in technology matters – AI, cyber, data, technology policy, enterprise technologies, digital transformation – on podcasts or at events in front of audiences of aspiring and serving board directors and Chairs.

This has been my path. Non-traditional career, non-traditional entry into the boardroom, non-traditional and varied ways for opportunities to find me, and vice versa. All in all, perhaps challenging to replicate.

Except the golden threads of curiosity and patience, and building relationships through creating value.

'Not quite the right fit'

Rudyard Kipling wrote of Triumph and Disaster, in his popular poem *If—*: 'And treat those two impostors just the same.'

His words are worth bearing in mind. All these 'successes' in being appointed to prestigious boards hide a much, much larger number of board conversations that variously faltered at long-listing, shortlisting, first interview, or second interview stages. From the board's side and from my side.

Board conversations are a two-way street. While there is rarely doubt that I could 'do the job', there is the critical question of a 'fit', which is how the interviewing board and I assess whether we can visualize working together.

Other directors' stories

Having met many inspiring and engaging directors, I sought more stories for lessons useful for those seeking to make a conscious career move to boardrooms.

From the stories of people who began serving on boards within the last decade, both those who have had traditional careers as well as those with non-traditional ones, there was one emergent trend: almost nobody stumbled into those roles. The 'why' and the 'how' both matter.

All had thought about their 'why? The stories shared with me surfaced many reasons. These included: seeking career resilience, a desire to remain engaged in the business world but not work long hours, a desire to serve, and at least for some, insatiable curiosity to learn and grow.

A senior executive in a well-known consumer goods multinational, who also serves as a non-executive director on an external board, described her motivation in these words: 'I am a believer in prosperity. I grew up in Morocco. My parents were middle class, civil servants in the ministry of health. Back then my country had a lot of poverty. So I am attached to the idea of prosperity and when you are on a board, you have actually a big impact on the continuity of prosperity, to make sure that prosperity is continued and shared, of course.'

Each 'how' was unique, albeit with some shared characteristics, showing how each path to the boardroom is unique, almost artisanal, not mass-produced or formulaic, and yet shares some similarities with others' paths.

Qualifications and certifications

Some have been purposive about broadening their horizons and gone about seeking unpaid roles or taking on formal qualifications such as board diplomas or certificates.

Do qualifications and certifications in Directorship matter? This question is often asked since there are many courses and qualifications on offer, some more expensive than others. Views vary.

Do qualifications matter in hiring? I have had occasion to recruit many board colleagues. Formal qualifications of a candidate were never a major factor influencing the decision. The judgement on whether the candidate could be a good colleague, bringing an open and independent mind and an additive point of view, always won out.

Do qualifications make for an effective director? Citing myself from elsewhere, I will say *governance is a contact sport*. Like swimming.

What this means is that it does not matter how well one knows the theoretical principle of 'nose in, claws out' being the board director's job, the real test is in the practice. How does one decide when the claws are almost out or the nose has not gone far enough? In what situations should the claws come out? How to balance challenge with support? No matter what course one attends and how mighty the price tag and label, this practice is best sharpened in the arena, the boardroom.

If matters are legalistic or regulatory in nature, directors can consult the company secretary (more in **Chapter 3**). They can also access independent professional advice. Stakeholder engagement, including regulator interface or activist shareholder engagement, is once again something one has to prepare for and then do, as demanded by a situation or circumstance.

A career arc of growing through seizing opportunities

Many directors shared stories of how throughout their careers they had taken opportunities with both hands, learning, growing with them, and realizing how many things they were capable of and experienced in.

One director spoke candidly and in great detail about his experience and life. In a headline his career might be summarized as '40 years in the tech industry', but these years covered leadership roles in many geographies. Early in his career, he worked closely with a first-generation entrepreneur; that business is now a global behemoth. 'It was a privilege, to be by his (the founder's) side, see things through his eyes, see how his mind worked, how he evaluated and made deals... I was privy to witnessing different angles he brought as a chairman,' he said. He credits that experience with igniting his lifelong journey in strategic thinking and good governance. His professional experience gave him wide exposure to 'different understanding of people, work, cultures, industries'. He described how throughout his career whenever opportunities arose, he did things outside his official remit. He shared two examples. First, asked by a mentor, he agreed to serve on an advisory board in energy security. This was far from the information technology industry in which he worked, but working with clients had given him the ability to learn about their business quickly and then to think creatively about how technology could help solve their most pressing issues. On a second occasion, he was invited to coach the founders of a university start-up. They were PhDs and, in his words, 'inventors not innovators'. He quickly found himself in the role of the executive Chair, navigating the divergent, often polar opposite views of the foreign investors on the one hand and of the founders on the other; there was also a huge strategic and international component. He served in the role for five years. Shortly thereafter, in landing his first major board role with a bank from an emerging market but listed in London, he was able to draw upon his extensive experience negotiating huge tech transformation deals with several global banks, his cross-cultural fluency, his communication skills, and his engagement style. 'There is no business now that is not a tech business', he said of their ambition, to which he could bring his insight and oversight. He then endured a long, gruelling interview process and regulatory clearance processes in two countries before being formally appointed.

Learning to assess and position one's skills

Aspiring directors are often told to think about their 'transferable skills'. That is incomplete, if not downright poor, advice. It is also perhaps better suited to changing executive jobs across industries than to making an executive to non-executive role transition.

More than finding 'transferable skills', aspiring directors benefit from 'metacognitive reflection'. What am I good at? What have I had to work hard at? What have I struggled with? How have I dealt with my strengths and my weaknesses? What has all that demonstrated to me about the values that have actually guided me versus the values I like to think have guided me? How can I make all this relevant to a board that I am interested in?

This is not to say that the pathway from executive suite to boardroom is fully dead. Executives, who have been boardroom-adjacent in their executive careers, or who have functional breadth and variety in their executive experience, seem to be able to make the transition to boardrooms smoothly. The catalysts for seeking change may vary from active pursuits of career resilience to a much-welcomed redundancy or voluntary retirement offer from the employer, the latter more numerous than one might think. CEOs still report experiencing some shock at being on the other side of the table in an oversight and not executive capacity. A former CEO, for instance, may find the ego adjustment as a non-executive a bit trying, sitting alongside colleagues who may have not been CEOs, but are now on an equal footing.

Anticipating and making the psychological shift

> A psychological shift is often the biggest change required in becoming an independent director.

Many directors across countries mentioned feeling lonely in their non-executive career. The loneliness appears to be exacerbated somewhat for those who abruptly go from having big budgets and big people management responsibilities to becoming a non-executive director with no budgets and no people to manage, from having a big titled job in a big brand employer company to working as an independent professional who must operate on the basis of their own value-add and reputation.

Directors also need to do significant independent self-development and 'homework'; a board meeting may be three to four hours long but the preparatory work may be several times that and mostly alone.

This may be why communities of directors are beginning to thrive in many countries around the world (see **Resources** towards the end of the book).

It is not the same totem pole the high-achieving executives have scaled, but a whole new totem pole and most have to start at the bottom. In a closed-door session hosted by a lead headhunter several years ago, the Chair of a European business group with operations in several countries shared her experience. She was a former CEO and had never had to look for an executive job. She spoke of how many people told her that when she leaves her CEO role, headhunters would be beating a path to her door to appoint her to boards. 'The phone never rang', she said, admitting her shock and advising people to get proactive.

More mundane issues of administrative support, such as diary management and logistics, also come up often. Senior executives, who in their executive careers have leaned on assistants for these tasks, find that smaller organizations often do not have assistants for them; yet others discover challenges in managing calendar invitations, board softwares, and often multiple emails and devices relating to different organizations in their portfolio.

Trust in God, but lock your car – the importance of due diligence

All directors I spoke with strongly recommend robust due diligence before agreeing to join a board. This can be conducted using a combination of publicly available information and tapping one's networks.

One director, who spoke with me, flagged the risk of a phenomenon where only partial information is shared, for which terms such as plausible deniability, sophistry, constructive ambiguity, or 'truthiness' come close but do not fit the bill. 'One must dig further no matter how impressive the crumbs of information sound,' he advised.[4]

Another director flagged the need 'to keep eyes open' in doing due diligence on an emerging technology; it is inherently risky and should always be challenged; and sites such as Glassdoor are helpful for cultural due diligence.

One of my interviewees underscored the risk of not being able to spend time on the due diligence when she was asked to join a board on a referral. The business that approached her had certain priors already fixed, and from her experience she knew the assumptions to be shaky at best. 'Voice your questions' is her firm advice, regardless of how you are being rushed and whether you feel relatively inexperienced compared to others in the room.

Real value is created when you shape your own view by filtering all the information through the lens of your own experience and knowledge. Do the risks match your risk appetite? Does the opportunity whet your appetite? Does something not add up?

Directors have an interest in protecting their professional reputations; red flags not discovered due to inadequate due diligence could damage or destroy reputations.

Reasons to serve:

I am interested in this sector, this business.

I can add value and contribute meaningfully, without needing to control all execution.

I get paid for my contribution or otherwise accept it pro bono due to the above two.

Reasons not to serve:

I am not interested in taking risks with my professional and personal reputation.

I do not want to lose control of my time and the structure of my life.

The current context of board service

Technology, climate, and geopolitics are the bigger themes shaping boardroom conversations but other trends are at play too. Those who advise boards and board Chairs on talent and culture as the dual engines of business longevity note that the last decade has seen a definite crystallization of professionalization of the boardroom. The 'tea and biscuits brigade' of the noughties is fading away. Increasingly it cannot be assumed that someone with an executive career reaching the pinnacle of a business can have an ad hoc chat with a golf buddy or a friend or a client, and land a board director role.

A former investment manager, and now Chair and non-executive board director in the investment sector, who has had a 50-year career in the industry, summarized the change beautifully: 'Over my career in this industry, we have gone from "my word is my bond" which was all about trust, to "trust but verify" which is more about good governance seeking assurances etc., to now "comply with this growing number of statutory requirements" which is basically about rules.'

Another director, who is both a senior executive in a well-known consumer goods multinational and a board director in Switzerland, spoke of how 'when you talk to the NEDs [non-executive directors] who are 70-plus, they spontaneously tell you, informally over dinner etc., how much it has changed. Because basically it used to be easy'. Interviews for this book suggested that still happens. The director mentioned watching a documentary about boards where they were talking about a word that really intrigued her: *pantouflage*.[5] The documentary, she said, was not talking about all NEDs, but high-profile politicians who transition from public to private sector automatically and easily into boards where they do not do much, and it is their image that endorses the company.

> 'Certainly the time I spend on boards does not look like *pantouflage*. It is quite the opposite. I look at the world right now I am just amazed, as a citizen, the cacophonies that we are in, the dissonant

noises, and the role of the board is to be the voice of sanity, to be brave. It is not about a fashion but a civilizational choice of justice,' she added.

Some experienced board directors argue that with growing strategic complexity, compliance burdens, and risks of reputational damage and personal liability, the talent pool available to boards will shrink. The reality – as interviews for this book showed – is shaping up to be different. Talent pools for boards are changing in their makeup, and growing in numbers, with more aspiring directors willing to step into the place of discomfort that are the modern boardrooms.

With board composition and expectations of a board director now very different, even from a decade ago, the way work gets done in boards is changing. Engaged and alert boards do a lot of work *outside* formal board meetings and formal agendas, giving far more time to the work than the advertised number of days, as nearly all directors I spoke with admitted.

What keeps some people discussing the burden of compliance, regulation, reporting, transparency, and public accountability is more than about the growing workload. This work demands full engagement, vigilance, and alertness because the risks arising from failure are real and very public. Most people are finding this change in workload challenging, especially for the relatively small fees that many board directors find themselves earning, some of them after highly remunerative corporate careers. Variations are huge across countries. In the USA it is not uncommon for a board director to earn US$250,000 or more; by comparison, in the UK a board director often earns less than £100,000, and many organizations and investment companies pay £30,000 to £50,000. Some don't pay at all.

And yet there are so many aspiring board directors, choosing to serve on boards. Why?

Boards are beginning to undertake skills audits, to meet the emerging requirements in skills and experiences, before writing the candidate specification for upcoming rounds of succession. This means many people, who have had careers previously seen as non-traditional, but who have skills and experiences and perspectives that are useful for guiding an organization into relevance for the future, are being considered for board positions. Aspiring directors also come to boards with a range of motivations.

It is evident that a churn is underway as to who will and will not remain in the talent pool, and who will and will not be willing and able to serve on boards. The real boardroom challenge is about future relevance.

Contrary to the earlier image of a board career as a 'retirement gig', which unfortunately is still the caricature presentation in media, board directorships are now a career in their own right. Board directors' ages are trending younger; board directors are more tech-aware, more globally sophisticated, more dynamic and culturally fluent. Your value to a board will be assessed within this dynamic.

The shift is purposive in many boards, a tad begrudging in others. The difference is easier to notice as an outsider than as an insider perhaps. It is however happening for certain.

Questions to consider

What are your reasons for wanting to serve on a board?

What is your credible, additive value for boards?

Which networks and communities do you feel you truly belong to? Have you built them already before you need them? How are you nurturing your networks and relationships?

2

The first 100 days

Experienced directors know that it takes three to six months before one can make meaningful contributions to the board meetings. The first 100 days matter. Here is how my first 100 days were spent in two separate phases of serving as a board director.

In my very first board role

My very first board role was as an executive director. I was the country manager of the Swiss subsidiary I had set up for my then-employer. Swiss laws required that the President of the board – the *Verwaltungsrat* or Board of Directors – be a Swiss citizen resident in Switzerland. The relationship between the Swiss President of the board and the country manager was governed by a clearly written contract. All this created an interesting employment situation – whereby my assigned 'line manager', who was the country manager of another European country office, had no legal power to fire me from my job; that was an interesting early learning about corporate structures and lines of organizational and legal accountability.

As an officer of the company, I was keen to ensure compliance with the laws – federal, cantonal, communal, as well as international – that governed business and life in Switzerland. Although my fluency in High German was deemed strong enough to earn me a dispensation from attending Swiss German lessons provided by my Kreisbuero or District Office, I was grateful at work to be able to lean heavily on the English translations of Swiss company and contract law, published by a leading chamber of commerce in Zürich.

For the first couple of months, while I was on a visitor visa in Switzerland, I met with the cantonal investment officers and then set up the legal entity. I made the case internally with my employer to establish an AG or *Aktiengesellschaft*[1] that needed more capital than a GmbH or *Gesellschaft mit beschränkter Haftun*,[2] but was better suited to the stature and status of the multinational parent company. Once the entity was established, it was possible for me to apply for my work permit. Until my own work permit was approved and issued, I could not work or do business development or do much more of anything else that might violate the conditions of my visitor visa. This derailed the 12-month business plan considerably. The irony, of being a person from India with its infamous Indian Stretchable Time, whose plans were being delayed in a country where everything works like clockwork, was not lost on me. It was an early lesson for life as well as business – that in new and unforeseen situations, things may not go to plan and a backup plan is always helpful.

The idea that 'culture eats strategy for lunch' was already around as a weak proposition. The experience of establishing a country office in a new market was my first taste of how laws and regulations get to strategy way before culture puts on its shoes, occupying the best table in the house, and carving out strategy in ways not always in the control of business strategists. A few years later I further explored this interplay of policy and strategy, culminating eventually in my doctoral work in political decision-making.

My first 100 days in my very first board role were spent navigating a new continent, a new country, and its laws and regulations, carefully picking my way through multiple languages and cultural nuances, keeping an eye on the revenue commitments on the business plan, while conscious every day of the many degrees of freedom and responsibility that came with my job. I was 26.

In my current journey on boards

Fast forward to 2016 when I formally began my current journey serving on boards. My first stop was a Board Apprenticeship with JP Morgan US Smaller Companies Investment Trust (stock symbol: JUSC), a listed fund with a portfolio of American small cap companies that have been the flag-bearers of American innovation. During my tenure on the board, we were to choose the tagline that describes the promise of the fund: *Invest in the Heart of America.*

The first 100 days here were quite different.

I was welcomed warmly to the JP Morgan offices on Victoria Embankment in London by a terrific set of board colleagues, a strong Chair, a competent company secretary, and a supportive relationship director from JP Morgan Asset Management. In the very first meeting, I had to step out for a few minutes while the broker discussed something confidential with the board. I later learnt that it was a discussion about the prospect of a corporate action.

My Chair invited me to spend time with her where she coached me on the asset class and the asset management industry; she had spent several decades as an asset manager and latterly as a board director and Chair. She taught me about the inflexion points in the industry's history and regulatory trajectories, the regulations becoming effective imminently (Markets in Financial Instruments Directive II or MiFID II, for those keen on more detail, bearing in mind this was before the UK's Brexit referendum that took place a few months later; MiFID II came into force in 2018), the changing makeup of the shareholder register from a relatively concentrated base of wealth managers and institutional shareholders towards a more dispersed self-directed retail shareholder base, the challenges arising from that shift as boards of companies struggled to connect with their retail shareholders, as well as broader trends shaping the investment industry.

Shortly after I began, it was time for the board to work on the annual report and accounts. Managing things carefully so as not to create a shadow director[3]-type situation, I was able to feed back to the Chair my thoughts on how an ordinary retail shareholder would perceive this section or the other. Unlike my board colleagues, I had not been steeped in the City of London for decades. I brought a fresh pair of eyes to the content, while also being able to observe and learn from the process of producing an annual report for a listed company.

I had three-quarters of a day dedicated to a formal induction organized by JP Morgan as the key service provider to JUSC. I was not treated differently for being a mere apprentice. Barring the portfolio management team based in New York, whom I had the chance to meet later in the summer, every critical functional lead – from company secretary, to compliance, audit, distribution and sales, and marketing – came and spent time with me, educating me on their role in supporting the board and the company.

In between these sessions, there was a knock on the door. It was lunch. For me. The JP Morgan kitchen had taken into account all my food intolerances. Duty of care in action.

It was truly a high value apprenticeship experience. In the first 100 days, I could not have foreseen how it would prepare me for the next 10 years on the boards of investment companies and other businesses. In hindsight, the potential corporate action discussion was perhaps a harbinger of things to come as nearly all my listed boards have seen considerable strategic action – a merger, an IPO, and an acquisition, to name the headline events as of 2025.

On a new board

The value of a robust induction on being appointed to a new board is sometimes only appreciated in its absence. The induction and onboarding process is a formal introduction to the scaffold, the 'skeleton' of the business. It is also something worth probing in board interviews because it provides insight into the board's culture in supporting and enabling new directors to start contributing.

In my experience, the value of a formal induction is enhanced if the new director takes the initiative too to understand the dynamics of the organization and, if new to it, of the sector, sector regulation, and regulators.

As more and more boards switch to using secure board softwares, a lot of useful information, such as industry jargon for directors new to the sector, past board minutes, and decision logs, can be retained in the archives. These can provide helpful organizational context. New Chairs of boards and committees can similarly review past executive reports and dashboards to see how metrics and reports have changed and evolved. I have benefited from these and recommend them strongly if your board does not already have these in place.

Some boards operate a 'buddy' system of peer mentoring, whereby a new director is paired with a longer-serving director who can help ease the new one in. Like all dyadic relationships, much depends on the two people involved. There are pros and cons, often discussed in directors' communities.

I have been a 'buddy' to two Board Apprentices. Each was clear-minded and curious, and I had no desire to influence them into being my 'friend'. I filled them in on context in between committee meetings (they attended committee and board meetings) and helped them with the questions they raised. We scheduled regular meetings and none of us dropped out of those. In my conversations with other directors, it emerged that if the assigned 'buddy' does not calibrate their engagement collaboratively, they could end up going over a lot of already-tilled land which is a waste of time.

Directors also rightly worry about the risk of inadvertently catalysing groupthink, where the buddies begin to identify too much with each other. It beats the whole point of a director's independence. If peer mentoring is on offer, it is worth making sure it works as intended, keeping enough daylight between the 'buddies'.

It is also worthwhile for new directors to have informal, one-to-one introductions to board colleagues, or committee Chairs, where the board is too large. In my experience, such an informal, social element helps new directors understand their fellow directors as well as executive teams better, as to their motivations, their tics, their interest or lack thereof, but also their politics, their values, and their prejudices. All this needs mutual disclosure and honesty to foster the trust that underpins working with the right balance between independence and the consensus-building essential to making board decisions.

Of course, nothing beats that old hat of Management by Walking Around. Getting to see the facilities, premises, and projects, while taking care not to barge in on people at work, always helps understand the pulse of the organization. I describe it as getting to understand the 'connective tissue' of the organization: connective tissue being less about *what needs doing* but about *how it gets done* and going *beyond process and policy* which I likened above to the 'skeleton'. Unfortunately, like in the human body, an organization's connective tissue is sometimes only appreciated in its failure to deliver. Most other times we just take it for granted.[4]

***

Experienced directors know that it takes three to six months before one can make meaningful contributions to the board meetings.

The first 100 days matter.

This is when, as new directors, we have the benefit of being the new kid on the block so to speak, bringing a fresh pair of eyes and ears to the boardroom and the organization. This is the time to observe, listen, and take notes on all things that seem to work and things that seem not to work. The more obvious something is, the more it is worth understanding 'why is it this way?' The answer will always be instructive. If used well, then by the end of the first 100 days, we as new directors will more likely than not have a mental map of the organization and understand at least some of its strategic strengths and weaknesses.

It is then time to get to work on the real job of being a board director.

Points to consider

Two eyes. Two ears. One mouth. Two hands. The first 100 days on a new board are a time to observe, listen, and take notes.

They are also a time to get to know other board directors and committee Chairs, perhaps in an informal, social setting.

If an induction is in place, it is worth taking it seriously. This is the formal scaffold of the business. If a formal induction is not in place, I have learnt to offer to help shape one, to ease the path for the future new directors.

तत्क्षेत्रं यच्च यादृक्च यद्विकारि यतश्च यत् |
स च यो यत्प्रभावश्च तत्समासेन मे शृणु || 4 ||

Listen and I will explain to you what that field is and what its nature is, how change takes place within it, from what it was created, who the knower of the field of activities is, and what his powers are. (Bhagavad Gita: Chapter 13, Verse 4)

The following chapter discusses the job of a director and of a board, essential and enabling structures so boards can work, stories of board dynamics from actual boardrooms, and finally the critical capabilities and relationships for successful boards.

3

Inside the boardroom

Popular culture and media depictions still take pleasure in portraying board directorships as jobs for the great, the good, and the outright grand, to fill up their leisure and retirement. If influenced by those, one might expect this section to contain juicy details of some modern version of *feriae conceptivae*.[1] For better or for worse, that does not describe modern-day boardrooms.

Conversations with board directors and Chairs, serving in several countries in Asia, Africa, Europe, and the Americas, suggest that the only moveable feast in modern boardrooms is the practice of governance which is evolving into true stewardship. Unlike the proclaimed festivals of the Roman times, most board calendars for meetings are set in the diaries almost 18–24 months in advance to allow for the fact that most directors have full lives outside the boardrooms which are far from retiring. These lives also must provide some flexibility and slack – there is a whole conversation about 'overboarding' of directors which will be addressed elsewhere in this book – for when there is a crisis or emergency that demands attention and time.

The emergency meeting in the 2011 film *Margin Call* is a good depiction of an urgent, short-notice board meeting in action. Albeit stylized, the scene features a rich and rapid debate that covers the gamut of pressing business concerns as well as ethical and moral questions, identifying risks and reputational fallouts. It also frames the firm in the context of the broader system and the variety of stakeholders who would face the impact of the decisions made in the room. It is instructive, though not an instruction manual. The next best thing is this book which adds to the conversation created and advanced by other excellent books in its genre (see **Resources** towards the end of the book).

Which brings us to the question…

The board's job, the director's job

What is a board's job?

A Chair speaking at an event on succession and talent on boards drew upon both his tenure as the CEO of a major defence organization, and his subsequent board directorships and chairing roles in engineering and finance sectors, and described the board's job thus: 'The board approves strategy, enables the executive team, and makes sure right resources are available, whether money or people.'

An insight from a former senior civil servant and CEO, now a board director in the UK, adds to that: 'Boards are not there for box-ticking on governance. They are in place to navigate the amorphous and do the hard job of seeking alignment to common goals.'

These two quotes capture the essence of a director's job on the board.

On the whole a director's job is made up of statutory and fiduciary duties. There are liabilities attached and repercussions that may arise. A board director may have access to some legal protections. The following pages offer an overview with which aspiring directors may wish to familiarize themselves.

Duties

While a board director is variously described as a 'critical friend' or a 'professional sceptic', the clinical answer to the question that applies in most jurisdictions around the world is that a board director's job is a combination of statutory and fiduciary duties.

Statutory duties are codified typically through legislative process, whereas fiduciary duties arise from common law or judicial interpretation as well as being shaped by corporate governance guidelines and codes of conduct. One provides consistency and stability, the other adaptability to the evolving circumstances in which businesses and societies operate. Indeed, the Law Commission of England and Wales has described fiduciary duties as '"legal Polyfilla", moulding themselves flexibly around other legal structures, and sometimes filling the gaps'.[2]

Conversations with directors in many countries around the world made clear that different jurisdictions see fiduciary duties differently and there are variations in the extent to which they are codified, in respect of the party or parties to whom directors owe legal obligations. For example, in the USA, Delaware law identifies three primary fiduciary duties: the duty of care, the duty of loyalty, and the duty of good faith; while in Canada, directors are expected to behave in the best interests of the corporation. Countries that follow OHADA[3] law have clear fiduciary duties of care and diligence, loyalty and avoidance of conflicts of interest, acting in good faith and transparency, as well as prohibition of certain types of transactions and financial misuse, e.g. receiving unauthorized loans, overdrafts, or financial benefits from the company.

Directors need to understand the codified aspects of their responsibilities but critically also need to keep abreast of their fiduciary duties, which may morph and change.

In my conversations with directors, we discussed similarities and differences between how statutory duties are codified variously in the Companies Act 2006 in the UK, the Companies Act 2013 in India, the Corporations Act 2001 in Australia, the Canada Business Corporations Act 1985 in Canada, the Companies Act 2015 in Kenya, the Companies Act 71 2008 in South Africa, the Swiss Code of Obligations, which has been in force since 1912, as well as codes effective in Singapore and the USA.

Directors' duties in the UK

The Companies Act 2006 in the UK codifies seven duties:
to act within their powers (section 171)
to promote the success of the company (section 172)
to exercise independent judgement (section 173)
to exercise reasonable care, skill and diligence (section 174)
to avoid conflict of interests (section 175)
not to accept benefits from third parties (section 176)
to declare an interest in a proposed transaction with the company (section 177).

Seventeen countries in Central and West Africa, constituting the third-largest single corporate law jurisdiction by surface area after Russia and China, follow OHADA law. OHADA was established in 1993; OHADA laws are referred to as Uniform Acts and they cover company law, commercial law, accounting, arbitration, uniform act relating to Commercial Companies and Economic Interest Groups (or uniform companies act) 2014 and security law effective 2011.

France being both the architect and a cornerstone of OHADA,[4] it is not surprising that, in the 17 nations following OHADA law, boards conduct themselves more in the fashion of many European boards. That is, they have two-tier governance (where management and supervisory boards are separate) instead of the unitary board prevalent in the Anglo-American model, as seen in Kenya, Nigeria, Tanzania, Zambia, South Africa, and the rest of Africa.

The influence of the colonial legacy on shaping governance structures and frameworks is unfortunately hard to miss. I would not dwell on that in this book and instead refer the reader to two excellent books on the subject.[5]

At the time of writing, the statutes widely seen as being most in flux for political reasons are those in the USA which include state corporate law, the Federal 1933 Securities Act and 1934 Securities Exchange Act, stock exchange listing rules, and federal statutes.

A regularly updated resource of Corporate Governance codes can be found on the European Corporate Governance Institute website.[6]

Liabilities and repercussions

With great fiduciary duties comes the great responsibility to discharge them, and the liabilities if one fails.

Shareholders in most jurisdictions worldwide can bring claims against board directors for negligence, breach of trust, breach of duty, or default. These liabilities can be extensive and cover, as they do in Canada, the broader general conduct of corporations. Statutory provisions often prohibit directors from being exempt from or indemnified against liabilities in case of such negligence, defaults, or breaches of duty or trust.

Repercussions vary too. Some shareholder losses can be made good through court-determined remedies or other interventions. Transactions and deals can be stopped by court intervention if director conduct is in question.

However, as directors operate in their capacity as individuals, they risk a lot more, such as being removed from the board or worse, being disbarred or disqualified from serving on boards in particular sectors or at all. The provisions for such disqualification of directors are often codified variously but the common reasons across jurisdictions remain related to a director's capacity to function (mental competence), financial solvency, delinquency, or conviction without or with elements of dishonesty such as theft, fraud, forgery, perjury, or misrepresentation.

Directors' disqualification in various countries

In the UK, directors may be disqualified by the courts, the Insolvency Service, the Competition and Markets Authority, the Foreign, Commonwealth and Development Office, or HM Treasury through the Office of Financial Sanctions Implementation (OFSI). Disqualifications may be made under Company Directors Disqualification Act 1986, the Sanctions and Anti-Money Laundering Act 2018, or the Counter-Terrorism (Sanctions) (EU Exit) Regulations 2019.

In India, directors may get disqualified and their Director Identification Number (DIN) rescinded for reasons including unsoundness of mind, undischarged insolvency, acts of moral turpitude which have been convicted and sentenced, offences under related party transactions, failing to make statutory filings, etc. (section 164 of the Companies Act 2013).

In Singapore, directors may be disqualified under several provisos in the Companies Act covering wrongful trading, fraudulent trading, or 'unfit' conduct. Various sections provide for such disqualification on account of bankruptcy, or by an Order of the Court, or due to the company being wound up for reasons of national security or interest, or due to being convicted of an offence involving fraud or dishonesty; or on account of three or more of their companies being struck off the register within a period of five years.

In South Africa, under Companies Act 71 of 2008, persons may be disqualified from being appointed as a director such as when prohibited by a court or any other public regulation from becoming a director; when declared delinquent by a court in terms of section 162 of the Act; when unrehabilitated insolvent; when removed from an office of trust on grounds of misconduct involving dishonesty;

or when convicted and imprisoned for theft, fraud, forgery, perjury, or other offences specified in the Act. A company's Memorandum of Incorporation may provide additional grounds for a director to be disqualified, e.g. failing to attend a certain number of board meetings. Section 69(11) of the Act gives a court a discretion to grant an exemption from being disqualified from appointment as a director.

In China, persons may not be allowed to serve if they are without civil capacity or have limited civil capacity; they have been sentenced to criminal penalties for corruption, bribery, embezzlement, or misappropriation of property, or for sabotaging the socialist market economy order, and fewer than five years have elapsed since the expiration of the period of execution, and fewer than two years have elapsed since the expiration of the probation period of suspended sentence; they have been deprived of their political rights for committing a crime, and fewer than five years have elapsed since the expiration of the period of execution; they have served as a director or manager of an enterprise that has been declared bankrupt and they bear personal responsibility, and fewer than three years have elapsed since the date of completion of the bankruptcy liquidation; they have served as the legal representative of an enterprise whose business licence has been revoked or that has been ordered to close its business operations due to a violation of law and bear personal responsibility, and fewer than three years have elapsed since the date of the revocation of business licence or the date of the order of closing down; and they have been listed by the people's court as the persons subject to the enforcement for breach of trust obligations because they have a large amount of debt, which is due but has not been repaid.

Protections

With it all being so onerous, why would anyone wish to serve as a board director at all? If you believe the chatter amongst directors of yore, few would.

And yet there are growing numbers of professionals, not just those nearing retirement but young, early, or mid-career professionals, interested in serving on boards. There are growing networks and communities of serving and aspiring board directors in many countries around the world (see **Resources** towards the end of the book). These communities help many professionals make the transition to their first boards and then support them on their journeys.

Governance is evolving into serious work, not for the retiring or the retired, but for those who are interested in bringing the benefit of their skills, experience, and knowledge to the cause of stewardship of corporations and resources alike.

As the role of board directors professionalizes and more demands are made of them, protections and support available to them are also maturing.

Directors have a right to seek, at the company's expense, professional advice on complex matters of compliance and governance and other relevant topics.

Directors can seek protection through several means – directors' and officers' insurance, indemnities, or ratifications by the company, and relief from courts. Dishonesty or unlawful actions of course cannot be ratified. To receive these protections, directors must be able to demonstrate that they discharged their duties with care and conscientiousness to the best of their abilities. Additionally, with increasing complexity and demands, directors can, if they wish, take out personal asset protection insurance.

Current and emerging questions

If boards have all these responsibilities and powers, it is valid to ask – '*Quis custodiet ipsos custodes?*' Who holds accountable those who are holding executives and managers accountable for shareholder and stakeholder concerns?

Shareholders and regulators are taking more interest in addressing this question. An organization's social licence to operate depends on the approval of one's customers as well as the broader public.

Shareholder activism is growing. This is happening alongside proxy advisers such as Glass Lewis, ISS, and others becoming more active in holding boards to account through voting advice upon which institutional investors rely.

Equally, other agencies are taking note. For instance, there have been recent instances of director resignations resulting from the Department of Justice in the USA taking a strong stance on anti-trust violations following too many directors being on overlapping boards, described as 'interlocking directorships'.[7] In the UK these sorts of board appointments bring directors' independence into question.

Another question that is rarely asked but perhaps should be asked more often is '*Quis curabit ipsos curatores?*' Who takes care of the caretakers themselves?

Opinions are divided on this question, as my conversations with several experienced board directors indicate.

Some feel directors, unlike employees, have far fewer rights. For instance, there is no right to sick leave or bereavement leave, and no protection from harassment. It is felt that directors are unsupported and often mistrusted or disliked by the executive teams whom they hold accountable.

Others are of the view that directors freely choose to serve in these roles and are legally on the job 24×7, albeit with huge flexibility, so there is no entitlement to any leave of any kind. They should, even under severe duress, be able to look after themselves and there is no duty of care owed to them. Indeed, in the course of the last decade I have known of several directors who stepped away with health diagnoses that may have made it hard for them to continue serving, and of others who underwent gruelling medical treatments and yet persisted in discharging their duties as directors.

An emerging provocation is – *'will an AI model be the next board director?'* This is an evolving space.

Generative AI tools are already being used by board directors for summarization, for further research into specific topics relevant to the business and its competitive environment, and for generating questions that boards can ask executive teams.[8] Of these, summarization is perhaps the idea that clashes most directly with the spirit and the letter of the director's job. It is our job as board directors, as professional sceptics, to read the board papers critically and in full, both to discover what is being reported and said, and to ascertain what we would like to see and what is not being reported. Attendant risks and biases also need to be managed actively. For instance, if a director is using a free or nominally paid, public version of a Generative AI tool, could they be exposing confidential information about the business? And if a director is using a private cloud instance of a tool, who is overseeing policies on access and telemetry to ensure the director does not overstep into executive territory nor compromise their own independence?

If statutes about duties of directors, regulations especially regulator interviews and demands for accountability, insurability of determinations made by the AI model,[9] and indeed technology to approximate judgement and explainable accountability, can all evolve rapidly to effect a wholesale change in the current governance context, then perhaps an AI model can be 'installed' as a board director. An interesting parallel can be seen in Albania, where a literal AI tool has been appointed a minister.[10] The stated goal is to eliminate corruption from public procurement. The 'minister', Diella, which means sunshine in Albanian, is being greeted with cautious optimism.

Boards report finding it challenging to keep up with evolving tools. For instance, Tiny Troupe, a large language model (LLM)-powered multiagent persona simulation tool from Microsoft, allows the creation of and interaction with artificial agents called TinyPersons.[11] These have personalities, interests, and goals, and can engage inside simulated TinyWorlds. Codifying the tacit and implicit aspects of human functioning and reading body language and other cues in the room that can change the tone and flow of a boardroom discussion are a whole different matter altogether.

Points to consider

A board director's job is guided by both statutory and fiduciary duties.

As an officer of the company, a board director has fewer rights than employees.

Almost anyone can serve as a board director when things are on an even keel; in difficult circumstances, the role of directors really comes to the fore to protect those to whom they owe a duty of trust and care.

Essentials and enablers of boards

Elements that make board meetings possible are quite similar across the continents. The maturity of governance models varies. How board meetings are conducted also varies. The complexity and dynamics of boards and board meetings vary by type of business (e.g. regulated), ownership (e.g. family-owned, private equity-owned, listed), size (e.g. start-up or scale-up, multinational), and geographical footprint. Increasingly, large businesses organized as Limited Liability Partnerships (LLPs) have started appointing external directors who are not directors in the statutory sense, but act as external independent directors bringing the same sort of scrutiny and support as they would anywhere else in a statutory director's role.

What makes board meetings purposive and effective is a whole different practitioner art. The following pages describe 'the scaffold' – the essential elements that make a board's functioning possible – and 'the building blocks' – the enabler elements that make a board effective.

The scaffold

The *Company Secretary*, also known as Board Secretary or Corporate Secretary or CoSec for short, is the linchpin of a well-functioning board. The CoSec is a governance professional and an officer of the company whose appointment and removal are board matters. The CoSec's role covers a wide range of duties such as keeping public records on the board up to date (including informing the markets and requisite regulators, ensuring websites are updated), filing accounts and annual returns, liaising with the stock exchange and registrars, undertaking compliance duties related to, e.g. data protection and data retention, and several administrative functions such as Directors' insurance and board payroll administration. The CoSec is also the record-keeper of board meetings and minutes.

Most directors learn quickly that a good CoSec is worth their weight in gold.

Many CoSecs specialize in their own sectors. The experienced ones have seen the arc of compliance and governance changes and can often answer 'but why is it like this?' questions without needing to trawl for answers.

Their experience in a sector and type of organization also shows up in how they write the minutes of the meetings, keeping in view liability and attribution concerns, commercial sensitivities, and other stakeholder and accountability considerations.

Minutes are the formal internal record of board meetings – of decisions made, the reasons they were made including points of consideration, key debate and discussions, actions agreed, and relevant background information. Minutes demonstrate how directors have fulfilled their statutory duties to shareholders and stakeholders, and declared conflicts and interests, and, if necessary, authorized them.

Many charities and public organizations publish their minutes on their websites. In such cases redaction for commercial sensitivities is a consideration. Ideally, the art of minute-taking will make sure the redaction does not reduce the minutes to an absurdity of black blobs. Similarly, many organizations are subject to public interest questions – such as Freedom of Information in the UK, the USA, Switzerland, and Australia, or Right to Information in India and in Kenya – and increasingly to subject access requests under data protection and privacy laws. Writing minutes takes cognizance of these considerations.

In the 17 countries in West and Central Africa that have adopted the OHADA system, it is required that board meeting minutes are made public, even for privately held companies.

And finally – 'write the minutes as if they will be read out aloud one day in a public inquiry or in court depositions' is a caution often joked about, but worth bearing in mind. If a board is unfortunate enough to be dragged into director liability lawsuits or other legal proceedings, the minutes, although an internal record, may be disclosed. Minutes are also disclosed during due diligence in corporate transactions.

It helps if those chairing boards or committees receive draft minutes as soon as possible – i.e. not one week before the next meeting – after the meeting is held. This allows minutes to be approved quickly and action points assigned as agreed, so that updates can be included along with meeting minutes in the papers for the next meeting. Signed minutes then become the official record of the meeting.

It is increasingly common that committee or board meetings get recorded, or an 'AI assistant' takes notes live. In any meeting, it is good form to inform the directors if a meeting is being contemporaneously recorded or otherwise noted. These tools, while convenient, create additional burdens for accountability trails and compliance with data protection requirements. For directors, it is imperative to understand whether these tools are exposing the organization's confidential information. Many board softwares now have in-built Generative AI tools; some offer customizable drafts and all seem to promise time saving and efficiency. The exact terms of use of these tools need to be understood correctly by boards. Directors must also understand how the AI tool is being hosted (locally, private cloud, or public cloud). Novel cyber risks may also arise.

A board that is not tech-literate is increasingly going to find all this challenging in discharging their statutory duties, but more on that elsewhere.

A well-defined, and regularly refreshed and updated *agenda* keeps board committees and boards functioning in accordance with their terms of reference and their strategic and oversight objectives. Agendas are pulled together by board or relevant committee Chairs in collaboration with their relevant executive team stakeholders. The Chair with the CEO, the Audit chair with the CFO and the COO, the Risk chair with the CRO and so on.

Agendas evolve and change to remain relevant. For example, when I was chairing an audit and risk committee, I worked closely with the COO to see if the next meeting's agenda was sensible or required change, and if so, how. Some dashboards were brought to us at every meeting and others at every other meeting. We also had a schedule for deep dives on complex topics such as fraud prevention, and they helped us understand the operational mechanics better.

What is already on the agenda is easy to see and challenge. It however takes something else to figure out what is missing. A director of a utilities company shared the story of how on a new board, she noticed that hardly any time was spent on a near-fatality experienced at one of the business's facilities. Despite being new, she brought the full force of her alertness, her depth of knowledge, her independence and – in her own words – 'her spine', to interrupt the swift moving-on and to ask further questions. Her intervention earned her a 'talk with the board chair' outside the meeting but she successfully managed to shift the board's perception of health and safety from a governance and compliance issue to a strategic issue failing at which could lose the business its social licence to operate.[12]

The length, structure, and content of the *board pack* and how far in advance of a board meeting it is sent are matters of much discussion in director communities. There is no set answer except to say it is horses for courses.

Large, listed, or complex businesses often have longer packs than smaller or start-up/scale-up businesses. The latter's boards often meet more frequently and therefore the size and content of their board packs is likely to differ from the former's. Without a formal infrastructure, a first-time founder team may well need some advice on how indeed to put together a board pack. Main boards versus subsidiary boards by necessity will have different board pack lengths and contents. Board packs around annual strategy review or half-year or annual results time will look decidedly different too.

Good board packs make clear which content is to be approved or ratified, which is to be debated and discussed, and which is for information or update. That is not to say the board cannot ask questions or seek clarifications to inform their points of view on any of these.

Board packs codify and present information to the board, but non-executive board directors always operate in an environment of information asymmetry. Whatever happens, the executive team will always know more than the board. Managing the asymmetry thoughtfully, sometimes diplomatically but sometimes fairly directly, is the biggest challenge in a board – one that may be taken for granted when the going is good but can become a big problem when things are tough.

Board packs hosted inside a containerized secure board software are increasingly common. Board software can also be used to retain in the archives any earlier decisions for context, previous dashboards to see how they have changed, and any other information that can serve as a reference or as an *aide de memoire*. It is also simpler to remove access to the board software for directors that come off the board.

Like all digital products and systems, board packs have audit trails and activity logs. In plain English, your CoSec or anyone with master access to the board pack can see things such as when a director opened the board pack, how long they stayed logged in, and whether they made notes etc. Shareholder and indeed non-shareholder lawsuits against boards are a growing risk. These lawsuits can be brought about for breaches of fiduciary duties, mismanagement, or fraud. Board directors should be mindful of not just minutes but also their own activity logs in the board pack or indeed their own notes being subject to a subpoena. Doing the work was never optional, but being able to show that the work was done may now be crucial. In a recent lawsuit in Australia, one of the directors appearing in the courtroom 'conceded he often relied on other directors to ask questions of Nuix management and hadn't read all materials prepared ahead of the February and March meetings'.[13] This was during a lawsuit brought about by ASIC[14] alleging Nuix directors had made misleading or deceptive statements regarding financial year forecasts for statutory revenue and for annualized contract value, and seeking declarations, pecuniary penalties, and disqualification orders.[15]

Meeting logistics – how often and where – are sometimes related to the agenda of the meeting. For instance, the experience of the start-up Chairs I spoke with and my own experience with start-up boards suggest that fast-growing start-up boards meet more often, monthly at the very least, and the meetings may be short in duration. This frequency and duration influence the size of the board pack, which may be relatively slim, and its contents, which may include updates on key metrics such as cash runway, commercial pipeline, customers onboarded, new hires etc., and issues for debate and board approval as necessary.

Pandemic lockdowns set an interesting experiment in motion. Boards found that they could function remotely. Some boards hired and onboarded new directors fully remotely. On one of my boards, I was made Audit & Risk chair during lockdown and started that role remotely. On another one of my boards, we served protective notice on the then-fund manager[16] and carried out the entire fund managers' 'beauty parade' during the first lockdown in the UK, before appointing a new fund manager[17] in the summer. In my experience as Audit & Risk chair, it was obvious to me that lockdowns and remote working had made it hard for auditors to provide assurances on matters such as occupational health and safety; they could not possibly visit employees now working from home in varying conditions, not all of which could be verified by employers. Several directors also found that employees had often moved to different locations, sometimes different states or countries, creating untold difficulties for compliance with tax and pension requirements for some employers.

Conversations with directors also suggest that the dominant preference remains for in-person board meetings. In the normal course of business, boards meet infrequently through the year and directors do not see other directors as often. Getting work done requires being present and engaged, listening not just to what is said but also reading non-verbal cues, which is easier in a physical space. Some directors on large boards noted that remote participation during lockdowns fostered disengagement and board packs not being read, ironically demonstrating how important it was that board culture and teaming were embedded in 'peace times' aka pre-lockdowns.

Since then some committee meetings have continued to be remote or hybrid. Indeed the transition – from back-to-back remote meetings that became the norm in lockdowns, to now trying to resist them and make time again on our diaries for travel to and from in-person meetings – is proving challenging for many directors. In such situations – and as I decided as Audit & Risk committee chair too – it may be more important to get quoracy and active participation than to enforce physical attendance.

Some directors expressed their discomfort with hybrid meetings where the chair must split attention between those in the room and those 'on the wall' or on the screen. The ones 'on the wall' risk being left out of the chitchat during breaks and need to rely on being called out specifically when they want to contribute, while the ones in the room feel the conversation is now stilted and has an artifice due to the adjustments. For all the conversations on inclusive cultures on boards, this topic remains sensitive and unresolved to some universal consensus.

Building structures helps the work get done in a board. Boards of complex, global companies and listed companies are organized for practical and statutory reasons into specific committees. Remuneration/compensation, nomination, audit, risk, finance and resources, governance, and increasingly technology, ESG, and marketing committees are in evidence. Some are required as prescribed by regulation such as remuneration/compensation, audit, and risk. Others facilitate work that needs to be done.

To be effective, it is helpful for a new director to understand how work gets done in a board. Is it done mostly in committees who then steer the board's decisions in particular matters, or does the whole board do everything? Does debate happen in the boardroom or mostly outside? If mostly outside, what formal and informal channels are used? Are these channels facilitating debate, or merely enabling decisions being made outside and brought into the board meeting as *fait accompli*?

A director of a complex, substantially publicly funded organization told me how committee Chairs on her board now had a WhatsApp group to communicate between meetings. WhatsApp communities of board directors are growing globally, providing an interesting window into the user sophistication with the platform.

Despite the promise that WhatsApp chats are 'end-to-end encrypted', a closer look reveals other challenges – for instance, individual directors may be backing up their chats but unaware that the backup is not end-to-end encrypted by default. The recent introduction of Meta AI into WhatsApp has also sparked privacy concerns as there are, as of summer 2025, several instances where the 'AI assistant' has helpfully given out unrelated private individuals' numbers in response to searches for helplines of business organizations.[18] If directors are sharing any confidential information on such informal WhatsApp groups, they risk exposing that information to Meta AI, a concern that can be mitigated in part by the new Advanced Chat Privacy feature. Meta AI itself cannot be switched off at all. Tools of convenience can very easily derail a director or a board that is not tech-savvy into places with indeterminate risk, and this point cannot be overstated.

Last but not least, *good chairing* is critical if a board is to function well. In business-as-usual (BAU), the Chair shapes the culture, sets the style and tone for the board meetings and interactions, manages the personalities around the boardroom table, and ensures good time management by keeping to the agreed agenda. In difficult times, the Chair leads from the front, managing the board while shielding the executive team to do the work needed.

> 'In simple terms, everybody leaves the board meeting feeling the organization is making progress or dealing with issues, and that they have contributed to the discussion and they have learnt something.'
>
> Mark Wood, Chair of Barnardo's and two tech boards

The building blocks

Building the board culture

Speaking with me for this book, the Chair of a listed investment company said: 'People think we are involved in the money business. We are not in the money business, it is still a people's business. People have to work well together whether it is directors on the board, or the companies we are investing in, or the asset managers. It is much more of a people business than people realise.'

Much has been written and discussed about psychological safety, inclusion, balancing individual independence with collective intelligence and consensus, resisting groupthink, and identifying and addressing biases as some of the elements of board culture. In a modern board the presence of these elements of culture removes the necessity for any director to have to lean on individual courage in order to challenge, clarify, contribute, or dissent; they indeed create an environment where all directors can think and operate not as agents of owners or shareholders, but as if they were the owners themselves. This mindset is especially useful when the board is faced with difficult decisions and must make sure the interests of all shareholders, not just the largest or the loudest or the ones with the most access to the board, are protected. These elements also help create space to accommodate different cognitive styles that may be present around the boardroom table (see **Chapter 7**) – the poet's style needs to be accommodated as much as the accountant's!

On boardroom cultures

'It is an English disease not to raise difficult subjects. People do not like it. Lots of boards therefore play in the margins, they agree things and go home.... Boards must cover all aspects of the business, not just bits and bobs.'

Chair who has led boards in the UK and in Asia

'The flip side of expertise is groupthink within that expertise.'

Lord Stewart Wood, Labour life peer, politics and economics specialist, and academic, speaking at Geopolitical instability and supply chain risk, Nurole's fireside chat, April 2025[19]

'I would say functioning boardrooms or good functioning committees, first and foremost, have to have a culture of psychological safety so that people feel comfortable talking about issues. And almost a corollary from there is to have a culture of having comfort with discomfort. It just means that people know that anybody who's asking a question is asking so that we could all do our jobs better and make a decision that's better in the long run, and nobody should be offended that a question was asked.'

Author on Nurole's Enter the Boardroom podcast, episode titled 'Decision-making: how boards make good decisions (and avoid bad ones)', available where you get your podcasts.

With so many components that need to work well, board culture cannot be created overnight; it must be cultured with deliberate intent, conscious practice, and regular reflection.

While structures and components of governance can provide guardrails as well as guidance, much of the board's culture is shaped by and manifests in behaviours – behaviours that are rewarded or encouraged but also behaviours that are tolerated or go unchallenged. For instance, if there is one director who talks over everyone, does not yield, and yet goes unchallenged in the boardroom and outside, the board is complicit in tolerating and encouraging the underlying disrespect or even the lack of self-awareness, and the resulting stifling of debate.

All directors need to have a shared understanding of the board culture. Board succession rounds provide an opportunity to reiterate the culture with an intent to strengthen it (where the board would seek a 'culture fit') or to revisit it with an intent to modify it (where the board might seek a 'culture add'). This is where the 'cultural antibodies' on a board are ironically also identified; bigger boards tend to hide them better than smaller boards.

Board talent management

Directors mention several considerations that influence and shape board talent management: emergent skill needs, regulatory and societal expectations in inclusion and diversity, board hiring processes and talent development, board construction, concerns about overboarding, and the influence (and opacity) of proxy advisers.

In an ideal world, all boards have a clearly defined strategy and undertake robust horizon scanning, which together help shape a regularly updated matrix of skills the board needs; the boards then run regular board refresh cycles finding perfect independent candidates, and everything is tickety-boo.

In reality, horizon-scanning can suffer from lack of agreement on what 'horizon' means; boards may operate from fear of missing out on the trend *du jour* (usually to do with technology-related topics); and diversity is often reduced to 'difference that meets the eye' rather than 'difference that needs discovery in the interview process and active management once the person is on the board'.

Some countries such as the USA seem to have no limits on directors' terms but have an age limit, while others such as the UK are quickly getting used to term limits and regular board refreshes. One of the most recent ones is Hong Kong, where amendments to its listing rules now deem that directors will no longer be considered independent after serving their role for nine years.[20] Independence is a key concern cited for term limits, although one listed company Chair said: 'These term limits are imposed from the outside, when shareholders really should take more responsibility. Are they reading the annual report and accounts? Are they speaking to the board? Active investors and fund managers and pension funds should vote their shares rather than lean on proxy advisers' recommendations.' This is of course a valid and important point. Often however, proxy voting and engagement are two different teams in institutional investor organizations, creating a disconnect between how they vote and how they seek to influence through engaging.

While improvements are being made in nearly all countries where I interviewed directors, most board roles still appear to be filled through referrals and networks. But where boards use external headhunters and search consultants, it becomes necessary to define the candidate specification. At the very least, the specification should distinguish between the 'essential' and the 'nice-to-have' skills being sought. It saves everyone time. If the specification says a horse is needed, then camels can save their time by not applying. The headhunter or search consultant can play a vital role in explaining to interested candidates how flexible the board is keen and willing to be, so candidates can make an informed choice about applying or not applying.

If the skills matrix on the board is regularly updated with an eye on current and future skills required by the business, and aligned with short- and long-term objectives, the specification will emerge from the skills matrix. Unfortunately, conversations with directors suggest this is often not seen as an important enough exercise to undertake regularly, at least annually at the minimum.

Diversity has remained a hot topic on boards over the last decade though facing headwinds in 2025. One Chair voiced his frustration:

> 'Hiring has become difficult. I understand the attractiveness of diversity. I always had women on my boards because women have different perspective from men and it is not sexist to say

> that because they have different lived experience of the world, different risk calculus, and a very different value add.'

This aligns with my view of how our independence is shaped – it is forged in our own experience, our own training, our own lived experience and everything else we are doing in our life. To be appreciative of that is probably one of the ways of discovering biases.

Another Chair was quite critical of automated systems. They 'are filtering out all the diversity we need!' he said in a Chatham House rule event.

> 'If you were to construct a perfect Investment Company board it would have an accountant, a lawyer, an investment company expert, an expert in the business the company is in, a poet to make our report and accounts interesting, and a physicist as they bring a different mental model. That is real diversity, that is real value-added. Diversity from a cultural perspective is a misdirection. Mainly because nobody extracts the value from that difference and it becomes a box-ticking exercise and you get a worse board because of it.'
>
> Chair of listed investment companies in the UK and in Asia

Diversity conversations nearly always veer into discussing hiring biases.

On that, Mark Wood, Chair of Barnardo's and two tech boards, shared his simple but powerful heuristic: 'If not, why not? Asking that surfaces the real objections to candidates. Often different adjectives emerge for men and women.'

While there is sometimes a risk that awareness of a bias can reinforce it, my view is that awareness of a bias also gives us a conscious choice. And then the choice we make reveals who we really are!

There's an active discussion on the use of psychometrics in board hiring. Far less time is spent on hiring board directors than on hiring CEOs, or sometimes even interns, which is in itself a debate. Most board directors I spoke with have limited experience with psychometrics; much of that comes from having done those tests themselves. Tools vary in their robustness and cost, and offer different things. Many administrators of the tools specialize in a handful of tools and very few have a wide repertoire so as to be able to explain the relative value of each and help a board select a tool for their purpose.

But like anything else, it has to start with the purpose of such tools. Is the board going to use psychometric testing for selection, rejection, and confirmation, or as an additional informational artefact alongside the CV, headhunter report, interview, and other tools in the process, or indeed for better management of the board after the appointment has been made? Once the purpose is clear – how will the board ensure balance between their collective judgement which is amorphous, and psychometric tools that may give assuringly definitive 'answers'? There is always the risk that if a candidate has seen the test before, they can easily game some answers and thus skew the outcomes. It is not beyond the ken of most generally smart people – which is the type boards often meet as candidates. Healthy scepticism is warranted. I recently did the Hogan inventory as part of a board recruitment process and I caught my own confirmation bias activating while the counsellor was explaining the findings to me, before showing me the written-up report. And yes, I was appointed.

Stakeholder interviews are one of the more interesting tools in director hiring. As a director on the board of a university, I was involved in the recruitment of the CEO. We used stakeholder interviews with academic and non-academic staff as well as students to assess how the candidates connected with their core stakeholder base. Most recently, the Chair of a well-regarded children's charity, which, he said, is run in governance terms as if it were a listed company, spoke of how they use stakeholder interviews: the candidates meet a panel made up of the children that are the beneficiaries whom the charity serves.

All these tools can be helpful to varying degrees and used to triangulate information elicited in the interview(s) and garnered from a wide range of formal and informal references.

Even with the most talented candidate, boards have to assess their capacity to do justice to the growing responsibilities and complexity of the board's role. 'Overboarding' however remains a sensitive topic for directors, with many feeling it is a blunt instrument.

Directors on overboarding

'Assigning a charity trusteeship one point, and assigning one point to a listed investment company board directorship, just goes to show that this institutional investor has no idea how much a charity board can demand in the UK. Let's just say even in BAU they are not comparable workloads at all.'

Listed investment company director in the UK, who has also served on a large charity board, commenting on a UK investor's scoring rubric

'Overboarding is a blunt instrument. If shareholders cannot trust us to manage our time, they should vote us off. Indeed if we cannot even manage our time, we shouldn't be on the board in the first place.'

Chair of listed companies in the UK and in Asia

Directors with experience of charity/NFP (not-for profit) boards point out that charities often do not have enough resources or a full slate of executive talent, requiring trustees or directors to do more work than advertised. One director shared her experience of chairing an NFP which demanded almost 1.5 days per week which she had to juggle with the demands of her full-time job as a senior business executive. Aspiring directors, who are still in full-time roles, might find employers often limit external boards to one non-conflicting or NFP board, which serves as a check on potential overboarding.

Countries vary widely in stipulating what constitutes overboarding too. For instance, in India, regulations limit directors to serving on a maximum of seven listed company boards, while in reality, the top 200 companies' directors hold an average of 2.1 board roles, according to Russell Reynolds research.[21] In Singapore, the Companies Act does not limit the number of directorships. In Hong Kong the recently updated guidance limits a director to six roles. In the South African experience, the pressure on listed boards to improve diversity means several directors seen as 'diverse' seem to be 'overextended'; research finds that 'compared to their non-overboarded counterparts, overboarded directors were better educated, had more specialised occupational backgrounds and had longer tenures on the boards on which they served', and recommends a case-by-case consideration of director overboarding.[22]

Proxy advisers and institutional investors set out their policies on overboarding.[23] At least some of these policies are highly granular, based on the principle of Different Types of Roles, Different Levels of Commitment. At the same time, *pantouflage*, as a director mentioned, or patronage-based board appointees continue to be on boards, sometimes several.

All these complexities of board talent management have made the job of the Nomination Committee chair – and boards – much harder over the last few years.

Conduct of the board meeting

An investor director who attends board meetings in investee companies in seven African nations, both in and outside the OHADA system, described board meetings in the former as follows:

> 'In Francophone Africa things are driven by a different legal system, the OHADA laws. Things are codified. The content that is discussed at the board meeting, the minutes are publicly available and become public record. These are private companies. And the records are publicly available. You have to go to the office and request them of course but (companies) need to make those pieces of information publicly available. That changes the dynamic.'

He went on:

> 'A board meeting in that context is typically a three- to four-hour event. But the official board meeting is only 30 minutes. You go through a number of regulatory steps, there is an officer who has to be present to make the meeting duly constituted and valid. And that person is only there for 30 minutes. And you don't capture the rest of the meeting at all.'

He concluded:

> 'The real meat of the discussion, be it strategy, finance etc., that all takes place outside of the context of the official board meeting. It is driven by this need to make your board minutes publicly available and you don't capture the strategy or challenges you are having. That makes quite a difference in strategy and approach. Versus what happens in South Africa or Kenya.'

Board meetings happen not just in a broad general context of good governance but how the procedural aspects are laid down too. The director cited above also highlighted that the procedural part of the meeting in OHADA countries is conducted in French, while the rest of the discussion can happen in English.

The procedural aspects of a board meeting of course include that it is duly convened, a Chair is appointed and – at least for the decision-making parts – the meeting remains quorate. In disengaged boards or committees, this can be a major challenge for the Chairs, as quoracy cannot be assumed. Sometimes the actual order of things may have to be different from that on the meeting agenda to achieve quoracy. If this happens too often, experienced directors see that as a sign of other challenges that need to be addressed, perhaps outside the boardroom.

It is in the actual conduct of the meeting that all the diversity and inclusion-related thinking comes to its practical test. Especially if the board is not homogeneous.

Alice Eagly's work, particularly on in-group/out-group dynamics and the social processes resulting, finds that social processes get in the way where the boards are less homogeneous and more diverse, leading to lesser productivity than on homogeneous boards.[24] Leung and Wang[25] also found that cultural diversity can suppress team creativity through the negative social processes it engenders. Their later work in a meta-analysis found that

> 'surface-level diversity in culturally diverse teams and team creativity/innovation are negatively related for simple tasks but unrelated for complex tasks, and deep-level diversity in culturally diverse teams and team creativity/innovation is positively related for collocated teams and interdependent tasks but unrelated for noncollocated teams and independent tasks'.[26]

These findings are of course not aligned with the popular discourse on the merits of diversity which cites better profitability and better share price performance. The purported merits are also an unfortunate but predictable outcome of eager advocates making the 'business case' rather than a full 'moral case' for the humanity of minorities, be it by gender, ethnicity, social class, disability, or some other measure, and then working to find ways to benefit from it.

Several Chairs pointed out that it is not simple to extract the value of that difference, that diversity. Chairing a non-homogeneous board meeting is therefore a far greater challenge than a board that is a homogeneous in-group. Alex Edmans's recent work on diversity in the asset management industry, undertaken at the behest of the Diversity Project in the UK, has unpacked the phenomenon.[27]

As Fiona Hathorn, CEO of WB Directors, now part of Nurole, put to me: 'A whole different kind of skillset is now needed, for a whole different kind of Chair is now needed for modern boards.'

Diversity is contextual – as under-representation depends on the social context. A few years ago, I was invited to speak about the Board Apprentice programme to a gathering of the great and the good in business. At the dinner afterwards, one of the business leaders mentioned he was a trustee on the board of a charity that works for sight, where all trustees except him were blind or partially sighted. I will never forget how he very calmly reminded the room that for his trustee board, he, who had sight, was the 'diversity' in the room.

Inclusion is practical – the skill and practice of ensuring that the value of all that diversity is realized. A dynamic practice to solve a challenge that is not static, one-time, or bounded. Pre-meeting work nearly always helps. And then in the room: how to make space for different cognitive styles? Who might have a relevant point of view to the knotty problem on the table? How to make space for different styles of engagement, and ways of sharing opinions and asking questions? How to elicit views without letting some voices dominate? Is there enough challenge and who might bring it? Where may friction arise and can it be harnessed for improving debate? Is there a lone voice? Are there signs of dismissal, disrespect, chauvinism, or subtle and unsubtle bullying?

As the main task in a board meeting is to debate, to discuss, and to build consensus, the dynamics of the boardroom are critical. Charity Chanda Lumpa, the former Chair of Zanaco PLC in Zambia, made the very important point – 'to disagree is not the same as to oppose', adding, 'Dissent in the boardroom, not in the corridors!'

Most chairs I have interviewed or heard at events make the point that the Chair speaks the least and the last. As a committee Chair I have tried to practise it as best as I can. The Chair wisely harnesses the analytical, the practical, the creative intelligences[28] – and with rapid change and complexity, I posit, increasingly the heretical intelligence – in the room, and drives the conversation to a conclusion, a consensus. A consensus that won't be undermined, weakened, sabotaged.

Governance as a contact sport

Governance is a contact sport. It almost does not matter how much one knows the theoretical job of a board director, the real test is in the practice of governance. Stories and experiences of experienced directors are great teachers as we navigate the ups and downs of this practice.

Most high-trust board communities and forums often share stories of experience and the lessons learnt so others can build on them. Many directors around the world have generously shared their experiences in candid conversations for this book. There can really be no exhaustive list of what really goes on in a boardroom.

Below are some of the most relevant themes that emerged from those conversations. For fun, they are organized into The Good, The Bad, The Ugly, and The Tricky, which can go any which way depending on how they are managed.

The Good

Retrospection and reflection

Boards approve strategic plans and review progress on agreed performance indicators at an agreed frequency, as part of BAU board meetings. Many directors and chairs, speaking to me directly or sharing insights at events, iterate that that it helps boards to have a board-only reflection at the end of every meeting. Unlike the board meeting, this reflection is often not structured and can yield insights on a variety of things.

Did the meeting go well? What could we retain? What could we do differently? Did we miss addressing something important? Did something emerge which just could not be pursued without derailing the meeting but that may now go on the agenda for later? Are we still discussing relevant topics?

While decisions come to the board for discussion, approval, and monitoring, the process of making those decisions itself is changing and becoming more data-driven. None of this is to suggest that boards were operating with guesswork before. Performance indicators after all are data. Things however are changing rapidly and perhaps so should the board reflection.

Organizations are now able to collect more and more data. Some of this data may not be useful or even visible – dark data – but its collection and storage raise data governance concerns. Data thus gathered may further be combined with data obtained from data brokers. That opens a fresh set of challenges related to data privacy. As businesses give shape to their Generative AI strategies and start to roll out implementation projects, it becomes doubly vital for boards to concern themselves with questions related to the data that is driving decisions.

In other words – effective retrospection of decisions is now inseparable from robust data literacy. To question the quality, completeness, relevance, and integrity of data underpinning the business intelligence, to examine and interpret data presentation, to ensure data governance is fit for purpose. Most of these capabilities require critical thinking and reflection – for which the board-only reflection provides space.

That brings up a question that boards should ask periodically if they do not already: are we fit for purpose, to prepare this organization for long-term success as it will unfold? The answer would make a vital contribution to board construction and succession planning considerations.

Board effectiveness

Board effectiveness is a result of how the scaffold and the building blocks come together in the service of good governance that enhances the long-term success of a business; success metrics typically are financial – revenues, profitability, and, where applicable, share price – or financials-adjacent such as market share, brand equity, and customer satisfaction. Other sector-relevant or business-relevant metrics may also be monitored. Conversely, board effectiveness is hampered by poor structures and group dynamics, which defocus them from their task of serving shareholders well and adversely affect their relationships with executives.

Recent surveys have found considerable executive dissatisfaction with their boards, including in their ability to remove ineffective or under-performing directors, their lack of preparation or time, and their members being on too many boards or too long in the tooth. A set of recent findings, in the fifth year since the first COVID lockdowns, shows executive appreciation of boards' ability to steer the companies through a crisis, although CIOs find boards lacking in digital, cyber, and AI oversight.[29] Media headlines do not pull punches either – the *Economist* called out the 'fecklessness' of some USA boards.[30] A 2024 piece of research by Law Debenture, a professional services firm, found that 'only 51% of UK workers actually understand the role of their company's board, a number which falls to 45% of those aged between 16 and 24'.[31]

How do boards assess their effectiveness? Short answer: through internal and external evaluations. Different countries' corporate governance guidelines prescribe various frequencies for such evaluations and whether they should be carried out internally or externally.[32] Both approaches have their pros and cons. External evaluators can cover a wide range of stakeholders with qualitative and quantitative approaches, observe some or more board and committee meetings, and can provide feedback and advice on, e.g. structures of committees, or how directors could improve relationships with executives and fellow directors. Internal evaluations are cost-effective but if the board has challenges with psychological safety, then more forthright comments may be held back.

An emerging discussion on board effectiveness is: *should directors be given individual key performance metrics (KPIs) or indicators?*

Some boards already do this. In the UK, some National Health Service (NHS) Trust boards, which are typically quite large, recruit for assigned specialist areas such as a director who leads on clinical topics or one who leads on productivity. The directors therefore are given objectives and evaluated against those using a mix of peer feedback and conversation with the Chair.

Other boards may pay similar attention to board construction. But it does not devolve to making any one director in charge of a topic, e.g. cybersecurity or ESG, as the flip side of such dependence is to make the person a single point of failure for the board. The board still bears collective responsibility.

Organizations are not collections of functional silos, and equally directors are now expected to be T-shaped, where the vertical stroke indicates their specialist area and the horizontal stroke is about their ability to engage with all the topics on the board's agenda. This is also more aligned with the reality of business, where functional and industry boundaries are blurring rapidly. With complexity and changes that need navigating, boards that remain agile and responsive can balance their scrutiny and support roles most meaningfully.

Setting KPIs for directors could risk becoming an exercise in chasing spurious metrics just because numbers look more certain and definitive, when the board directors' job is largely amorphous and emergent in situations.

Personal effectiveness as a director aka Heraclitus in the boardroom

Can one learn how to be an effective board director? If so, how?

Speaking at a closed-door event, the Chair of a port in the UK said: 'The more you do, the better you get.'

Wisdom attributed to Heraclitus[33] – no man steps in the same river twice, for it is not the same river and it is not the same man – encapsulates how most directors experience their own growing effectiveness. There is constant learning through experience on different boards, calibrating their own balance of technique, i.e. the practical aspects of making decisions, and skill, i.e. the capacity to do something well. Directors seeking to remain relevant also continually upskill in emerging topics in technology, regulation, and other factors in their business environment. This both follows from and strengthens my view stated earlier about the value of metacognitive reflection that benefits the effectiveness of both aspiring and serving directors.

The Bad

Lack of understanding of the board's job

Across sectors, directors raise concerns about first-time board directors who do not understand their job. A CEO, who had a productive and supportive relationship with her Chair, said she realized in her first job as Chair that she would have to educate and coach many of the board colleagues she had inherited.

This is not a problem limited to less experienced or unskilled directors. Several CEOs, who spoke with me, lamented former CEOs who joined their boards as non-executive and then wanted to control the CEO or direct the CEO to run the business as they would have run it. 'They shouldn't have left their CEO role to become a non-executive director, their thirst for control had not been quenched,' said one such harassed CEO.

Highlighting another flavour of the problem, a Chair in both not-for-profit (NFP) and for-profit sectors said: 'In NFP, there is often a lot of activity reporting, low information gunk. Sometimes I see the CEO report and think, "this is what you would say on open days, not in a board pack". Where is the answer to the so-what?'

First-time board-adjacent members of the executive team often also need coaching in understanding what the board does and how they should engage with it. One director shared a harrowing experience: as she was seen as accessible, a new member of the executive team started to engage with her, quickly escalating to blaming her for perceived 'poor board decisions' on matters that did not come to the board at all. The director had to make a decision quickly. She decided to coach the executive on the scheme of delegation active in their board, pointing the executive team member to governance materials, and then having to turn the dial down on looking 'accessible'.

Unmanageable board

Unmanageable boards often illustrate the *Anna Karenina* principle – 'Happy families are all alike; every unhappy family is unhappy in its own way.' The examples below come from conversations with directors in different countries, which suggests this may be a universal challenge.

One attribute may be an unmanageable size, usually too large.[34] A highly experienced senior director in the higher education sector noted how UK university boards are weighted by historical baggage, with a royal assent or charter shaping their governance, growing statues and ordinances, and sometimes 20 or more people on the board. 'Many lay members are not on the board based on skills, too many unqualified people are trustees and directors. The board packs are huge. A two or three hour meeting with 20 or 25 people in the room. The maths just does not add up!'

There may be more than one way to address the large size challenge – where feasible the chair could take a hard stand on reviewing the size of the board.

Sometimes such shrinkage is not permissible. For instance, in Germany there is a legally mandated minimum number of directors on the supervisory board depending on the size of the firm; in South Africa, the King III report[35] recommends that a board should have more non-executive directors than executive directors; in the Netherlands, large companies are required to have at least three non-executive directors; and in the USA, independence and committee requirements imposed on listed companies make it necessary to have at least three non-executive directors. Indeed, in the example quoted above, there may be historical reasons or provisions in the articles or governing constitution that make it hard to change the size of the board. In such situations the board has to organize its structure and work for effectiveness.

On the other hand, boards can also be too small, so there is no scope for debate or dissent, e.g. a start-up board with investor directors but no independent director or chair.

Another attribute could be disengagement or passivity of some directors. In one situation, a board had a director who was a political party candidate. While that was not prohibited by the board's terms of reference, the director was frequently absent, and when present, appeared not to have read the papers and made irrelevant comments. Other directors approached the chair to request an intervention as those behaviours were deemed distasteful and disrespectful by the more engaged directors.

Other imbalances also make boards challenging to run – dominant voices, attempts at capturing the board's decision-making by forming cliques, groupthink through cognitive laziness or disengagement.

A board that has several directors engaging frequently and regularly in undocumented communications on the sidelines, outside the board, and without a trail can derail the functioning of the board. Cliques that form can isolate new directors especially, reduce director independence, and potentially capture board debate, rendering it a farce. Information may be traded outside the boardroom and decisions made informally. Such interactions create significant information asymmetries, enforce biases, and undermine trust.[36]

These are not uncommon challenges. While they are laid at the Chair's door to address and resolve, all directors unimpressed by these dysfunctions should consider how they could help the Chair in breaking the doom loop.

Executive and board mental health and well-being

A 2022 Deloitte survey of 2,100 employees and C-level executives across the USA, UK, Canada, and Australia found nearly 70% of the C-suite are seriously considering quitting for a job that better supports their well-being.[37] The 'serial CEO' is also increasingly less common.[38] As the former CEO of a well-known British bank said in a private event: 'Friday night calls? Always bad news. For the CEO and for the Board.'

Executives' physical safety and physical health have been on boards' risk radars a long time. With the unfortunate upward trend in recent years of executive and founder deaths by suicide, executive mental health is increasingly a concern and a risk to manage too.

Both compassion and good governance require that boards ensure the provision of the right policy and support mechanisms, such as helplines for employees. However, it gets complicated where a board director's mental capacity is under stress or diminished.

As discussed in the box on page 32, some countries, such as India, have laws that disqualify directors on the basis of mental capacity. In other countries, such as Kenya, contract law restricts an individual's capacity to contract on grounds of mental incapacity. Australian courts on the other hand have found that 'incapacity in one area does not automatically mean that capacity is lacking in another area'.[39] This is a nuanced issue demanding the board exercise caution and good judgement.

Should a board intervene if the CEO or another executive are showing signs of duress and reduced capacity to function?

The answer to that is a qualified 'yes'.

Yes, because the attendant risks of inaction can be numerous and serious. It is not just about the executive's capacity to work, but also about any potential misconduct arising from the stress, as was seen in the case of AA Insurance's former CEO and Chair's dispute with the company[40] in the UK, or disability arising from such a situation.

And 'qualified', because legal advice on the matter is necessary to get the intervention right to protect shareholders and the company, but also to execute the board's duty of care towards the executive in question.

With the Chair–CEO relationship being critical to the success of the company, the Chair may be the first to notice the need for an intervention. It is best not to ignore the signs.

That said, board directors themselves are not impervious to stresses, especially in ugly or tricky situations. Different individuals bring different levels of resilience and self-care – and even their own lens on deontological or teleological view of their duties as directors. The recurrent message from experienced directors is to lead from personal integrity and purpose, and while sometimes courage is the main resource needed, it helps to know like-minded director colleagues whose presence in the room can be supportive.

The Ugly

> 'Stressful situations reveal real character.'
>
> Chair in engineering and finance sectors

Boards have to step in and step up, often in unpredictable ways, when a crisis hits. Crises can be variable in scope and impact. They crystallize rapidly, whether in a sudden emergence, e.g. a cyber attack, or when a slow-burn issue suddenly becomes too big to ignore, e.g. bullying on a board causing a breakdown or bringing about a lawsuit. They reveal fractures and fault lines in culture, processes, controls, systems, and internal and external communication, and can create a cascading failure. They extract a price – financial, relational, reputational, sometimes existential. When resolved, there may be seminal lessons as well as repair opportunities both for the organizations and for individuals.

The 140-year-old retailer Marks & Spencer (M&S) is a British national institution. In April 2025, cyber criminals successfully gained access to its systems using social engineering tactics via a third-party supplier.[41] The attack disrupted the business's operations, customer data was stolen, and the disruption lasted a few months. The financial cost was substantial, with a £300 million hit to profits and almost £750 million wiped off its market capitalization.

How was the crisis handled? It was noted that the business had war-gamed and was prepared for the crisis. Early steps such as the CEO's transparent video statement[42] and the staff working to help customers were appreciated;[43] delayed disclosure of the breach and exfiltration of customer data not so much.[44] Emails were sent to consumers in May 2025. I received one too.

Indeed, I found this part of the consumer communication worth reflecting on:[45]

> 'Unfortunately, the nature of the incident means that some personal customer data has been taken, but there is **no evidence that it has been shared**. The personal data could include contact details, date of birth and online order history. However, importantly, **the data <u>does not</u> include useable card or payment details, and it also <u>does not</u> include any account passwords**. For more detail, see our FAQs.'

This communication seeks to draw attention – by the use of bolding and underlining – to something about which a consumer should worry far less in this incident. Payment cards can be replaced trivially easily and passwords can be changed quite simply too. The real risks to a consumer come from someone now potentially having access to their name, their date of birth, and their address from their order history. In combination, this data is perfect for identity theft, and financial fraud and losses being visited upon a consumer.

Communication during and after a crisis is critical – with respect to timing, tone, and content – and should have board oversight to support the executive as well as to watch for risks arising.

A globally experienced director shared the story of a listed company in a vital and growing industrial sector that went from thriving globally to collapse in a space of one year. As a new director on the board, she witnessed the decision to fire the CEO and soon after, the CFO; the chair and the audit chair stepped into the respective interim roles. Both were capable and experienced but not exactly suited to the roles in a company that needed agility and financial discipline. She then led the search for a new full-time CEO. Despite a strong new CEO and a round of fundraising, where the board invested too, the company collapsed within a year.

Reflecting on this experience, she said that while as a new director she did not have social capital in the business, she carried a large responsibility for CEO search. She could draw upon her experience as a globally experienced former executive in large corporations across telecom, industrial, and consumer retail sectors. While the experience was not pleasant, and the directors lost money, she feels it was good experience and she now feels braver; even as a new director, if there were a crisis, she would rely on her understanding and experience to challenge or to say that a different decision is needed.

Discussing a whistleblowing complaint coming straight to the board, a director, who has extensive experience in people and talent, spoke of raising it to the chair, advising him that the organizational process must take its course and the board should not be the first port of call but an escalation mechanism. Yet another director in a large, publicly funded organization found that the nature and scope of the whistleblowing complaint quickly showed the inadequacy and limitations of their organization's process; the board director had to step in, seek extensive legal advice on a substitute process, and manage an arm's length independent investigation of the allegations. Extensive regulator interface, the need to maintain confidentiality, and the relentless stress took a massive toll on the director's health. A full process overhaul followed but, dissatisfied with the outcome of the investigation, the complainant sued the organization claiming damages anyway.

Other challenges, such as hostile corporate action, activists building stakes in the company and precipitating ownership battles, and activist shareholders seeking extraordinary meetings and seeking board seats may also arise. How should boards handle these challenges? Speaking at a closed-door event, the Chair of a listed company said of such times: 'The board is ultimately the conscience of a company.'

The Tricky

The Tricky can get good, bad, or ugly depending on a whole host of factors within and outside the board's control. An experienced board director, speaking at an event about boards facing turbulence, articulated why boards should care and be diligent in such times: 'Reputation is the non-exec's currency.'

Corporate action (M&A)

Whether the company is making an acquisition or being acquired, the Chair and the CEO carry much extra workload, although that can easily trickle down to the whole board and overwhelm the executive team who are also charged with BAU.

A Chair, who described himself as a 'serial acquirer' by virtue of having led over a dozen acquisitions and a couple of disposals, outlined the key fits to seek as being strategic fit, cultural fit, and financial fit.

It is worthwhile, as an acquirer, to visualize what things will look like after the deal has completed – whether the acquired entity operates on its own, as a hybrid, or as a fully integrated unit. In a conversation, the Chief People Officer of a scale-up, which was acquired by a huge global company with a slow, safety-first culture, observed that the 'bear hug' of the latter felt suffocating, and expressed concerns that if and when the acquired scale-up aligned fully, its lithe and agile culture will change completely.

By the same token, ignoring cultural fit, losing the attention to detail, whether financial or otherwise, and smugness or complacency on either side of the transaction are unhelpful. Speaking at a Chatham House rule event, an experienced director spoke of his experience of a cross-border corporate transaction. If successful, it would allow a privately owned USA business to list in the UK via a merger into the London-listed entity. He described how, despite solid experience in the executive team, the UK board found escalating demands on their time and the company's costs challenging; the UK board had to educate the USA folks on the demands of listing in London, and deadlines made whooshing sounds as they flew by, as advisers on both sides continued to disagree and banks got unhappier. When the USA party's desire to install a Chair both as CEO and CFO was made known, the UK board had to be very vocal and firm about UK listed company governance. The transaction was made more onerous than it had to be due to cultural incompatibility, time zone challenges, and regulatory and compliance challenges. In the end, the USA party pulled the plug, forcing the UK entity into a parlous state which the board had to further work assiduously to resolve.

An M&A muscle is often not a developed muscle in most businesses, but as these are strategic transactions, it helps to develop a clear point of view and prepare a structure as a strategic resource; clear roles and responsibilities between board and executive team help balance BAU with the transaction.

Managing conflicts of interest

'No conflict, no interest': I don't recollect exactly who first said this to me, when, and to whom it was attributed. Although glib-sounding, the adage has a grain of truth. 'If you want to add value you have to care deeply about the company and its business,' advises Fiona Hathorn, CEO of WB Directors.

Most directors serving on a board have some degree of interest in the business they are scrutinizing and are quite likely to come from the sector or service providers to the sector. So just as there is no true Scotsman, there is likely no truly non-conflicted director.

A conflict potentially arises when a person's personal or professional interests raise doubts about whether their judgement and/or their decision-making will be free of biases created by those interests, and therefore whether they can potentially harm the interests of the company and its shareholders or stakeholders. In other words – it is a potential conflict when the economic and other interests of a person are not aligned with the economic or other interests of the company or charity they oversee.

These conflicts could be financial in nature – which are slightly easier to identify – or non-financial, but both kinds bring doubt upon the director's loyalties and ability to serve their fiduciary duties impartially. Sometimes it is quite simple, e.g. one just cannot serve on the boards of two companies that are competitors in the same segments in the market. Or a person in an executive role in Bank A can be quite certain of not being allowed to serve as a non-executive director on the board of Bank B, as a friend of mine found out; I had warned said friend of the conflict when the board role was under consideration. Sometimes Chairs of boards may permit such appointments. However, proxy advisers, who influence shareholder votes in listed companies, may not take the same view.

Conflicts of interest are not static, because people's personal and professional interests evolve. Conflicts must therefore be probed before every board or committee meeting, specifically as relevant to the agenda of that meeting. Conflicts can also accumulate, accrete, and carry over from past involvements. It was reported some years ago that NHS Digital had spent 15% of its budget with Accenture, where two of its board members worked earlier and where they had shares.[46] Some of the minutes of their meetings are public and include conflict-related comments, but their process of managing the conflicts is not minuted. Regardless, the optics of conflicts of interest is not good.

The materiality of the conflict is a tougher one. A wide variety of things, such as shared directorships or former or current contractual or employment relationships, can be captured on information sheets or formal disclosures. These are usually professional interests and rely on self-disclosure. Increasingly however, it is not exclusively professional interests; e.g. in the UK, the Financial Reporting Council's register of interests includes information on spouses' and family members' jobs, and pension entitlements from previous jobs, especially audit firms' pension plans.[47]

But there is a wider variety of things that cannot be captured on information sheets. 'Vested interests' rather than the clinical-sounding 'conflicts of interest', if you will. Is the CEO the godparent of the Chair's child? Are any directors old buddies of the CEO? Which directors shoot or fish or golf together regularly, thus opening backchannels and rendering the board susceptible to capture? It starts to get murky quickly. At the same time, the impact of such vested interests is harder to identify and prove, and hence manage.

Assessing the scope and materiality of the interests – as well as avoiding the finite risk of throwing the baby out with the bathwater in an over-zealous attempt to eliminate all possible conflicts – requires good judgement.

Experienced directors agree that the source of conflict, the disclosure of conflict, and its materiality are all critical. What is most important though is management of conflict. Transparency and communication are vital here.

Publishing the board or committee agenda, clearly spelling out what decisions may be made at the meeting, enables conflicted directors to recuse themselves appropriately and not try to influence decisions where their vested interests are implicated. If need be, independent directors can play an active role in managing such conflicts. In listed companies, independent directors can approve a conflict under some conditions.[48] Regulations can also help manage conflict by prohibiting certain activities, e.g. in listed companies, directors in possession of undisclosed material information are not allowed to trade shares for certain durations of time; these regulations also cover their related parties, e.g. their spouse or children, who could benefit from having access to such information and trading on it.

Conflicted directors can still contribute their expertise to the debate and discussion and it is to some extent on them to manage their biases in their contributions. The Chair of the board or the committee can then ask them to step out and have that minuted. The commercial decision can then be made without the conflicted director in the room.

This tightrope walking makes chairing a tough gig, one that is worth getting right.

If all else fails, it is worth visualizing what it might be like to clean up the mess resulting from being on the front pages of your country's most circulated tabloids for all the wrong reasons. It should focus the mind instantly.

Handling disagreement, recording dissent

A board is an assembly of peers, and if constructed well will pull together a range of people with different lived experiences, cognitive styles, temperaments, mannerisms, and networks. A wide variety of conflict and disagreements can and do arise. It is not uncommon for directors to dissent and for that dissent to be recorded in minutes.

In **Chapter 1**, we saw the experience of a director, serving as executive chair of a start-up, managing the polar-opposite views of the founder-CEO and the foreign investors. Getting new investors on the cap table[49] can cause a lot of stress in such companies. Other chairs of start-ups or PE-owned businesses have had similar experiences. By no means are these situations limited to start-ups or founder-led businesses. All conversations suggest there is no substitute for investing time in getting to understand people and their motivations and styles. It helps pre-empt disagreement and potential conflict.

An experienced chair simply advised: 'Soothe anger ahead of meetings so the meetings can be managed.' Another said: 'I just had to find the courage of my convictions to deal with an aggressive investor director and did not get a major outburst but it could have been uglier.'

The recurring theme: a lot of work in such situations is done outside the boardroom or formal meetings. However, directors have legal duties and the disagreements need to be resolved, and sometimes those legal limitations can serve as guardrails.

Dissent however is different from disagreement. Dissent is a divergent view, and a more profound and principled objection.[50] Unless it is recurrently disruptive and vexatious behaviour, which must be addressed differently, dissent must be recorded, especially if a major decision in a board has come to a vote and a director wishes to withhold their support of the consensus on grounds of ethics or morality.

Ironically, the voicing of dissent can be a positive signal – of a board culture which provides psychological safety and earns the trust of directors, of board dynamics that provides space for differing points of view, of a board director who cares about the company enough to share what they see others missing, trust and courage both needed, and of the board's leadership.

If however the dissent is recurrent, and comes from different directors, the board needs to reflect on what may be going wrong.

Easing a director off the board

There are occasions when a director has to be eased off a board, outside their term end or shareholder vote at the general meeting. Typically this comes to pass when a director is seen as disruptive, for instance a director who is a non-executive but behaving like an executive.

The chairs and directors I interviewed mentioned a range of tools to address this – 'buddying-up' the disruptive director with someone more experienced for feedback, peer-mentoring, getting support through an external coach, or getting direct feedback from the Chair.

There is also the occasional director who does not step up to the plate. This is seen as a more addressable challenge. A variety of approaches – external coaching, skills assessment, and skills training especially in governance, ongoing feedback in one-to-one sessions – are used. One Chair suggested 'taking stock of their life as a whole' as they could well be experiencing stressful circumstances elsewhere and needing support.

It all however comes down to pulling the trigger and doing so fast, as not solving it could send the wrong signal to others on the board. The manner of easing off needs delicate handling. The director may be allowed to continue till the end of their term or may resign, but a narrative is agreed upon to explain the unexpected departure.

Prevention however remains the best medicine and one Chair advised that a robust selection process, including obtaining a wide range of formal and informal references ahead of the director's appointment, may reduce the risk of having to ease someone off the board.

Seeking balance dynamically

As a non-executive director, one is constantly seeking balance. Given the dynamic nature of boards and the situations they deal with, when they go beyond box-ticking and compliance, it would be fair to note that balance is not a static entity but a dynamic exercise in being responsive to events and changes.

Some of the balancing acts, that are part of board service and that can go well but equally easily go wrong, include balancing 'critical' with 'friend', 'accountability' with 'advice', or 'challenge' with 'support'. The stories shared in this book illustrate various instances of this balance-seeking.

The risky business of horizon-scanning

In a well-functioning board, a blank-sheet, tabletop exercise in identifying emerging risks and opportunities for the business – aka horizon-scanning – can be a very effective way to keep reminding ourselves of the focus on the 'long-term' part of the directors' job of ensuring the long-term success of the business.

It can be tricky to get right.

How far is the horizon that we are scanning? Not being prescriptive about it at the very beginning may help bring out some interesting views, although directors should not limit their thinking to their own remaining tenure of service. In the discussion that follows, timelines can be aligned more clearly to ideas to ascertain what may come to pass in the near-term and what seems further away.

Do we see the dark cloud or the silver lining? Undertaking blank-sheet, tabletop exercises in identifying emerging risks for a business can quite easily become an exercise in identifying whether we err on the side of 'knowing' or on the side of 'hoping'. In shaping the future of leadership and governance, or even just seeking the answer to 'what do I say to my children today?', a good dose of reality admixed with hope is necessary.

Are we able to look past our own smudged lenses? A blank-sheet risk-surfacing exercise is not meant to be an exercise in rearranging the deckchairs of our biases, but one that challenges our opinions, widens our horizons, makes us look up, and pushes our imagination and esemplastic thinking.

Two insights stood out in my conversations with experienced directors.

The Chair of a higher education institution pointed out: 'Organizations can cultivate institutional apathy. The temptation is to optimize, to tinker. [There seems to be] No imagination, to zero-base and be bold, apply design thinking, especially as we face a transformational opportunity with AI.'

A listed company director in the UK described the work: 'I have thought about the difference between foreboding, foreseeing, and threatening. Boards and leaders need to heed the first, be able to engage with the second, and call the bluff on the third.'

There is something to be said about the need to distinguish between people who keep an eye on emerging phenomena and small data signals and connect a lot of dots, and people labelled as 'conspiracy theorists'. The former can usually unpack their thinking if they are asked, the latter perhaps not.

Capabilities and relationships

Directors almost universally agree that there are some critical success factors that make a functioning, effective, and successful board possible.

The Chair

Whatever the ownership context, listed or private, owned by family or private equity, or indeed a public body, a good, capable Chair of the board is key to the company's success. They are the main contact with the key shareholders and stakeholders, set the board's agenda, ensure there is enough time for discussion and debate, and ensure that the board is fit for purpose (using a variety of tools directly and through committees, including board evaluation and board succession planning). In other words, the Chair runs the board.

If something has to change on a board, the Chair is fundamental to leading and driving that change.

While the Lead Independent Director or Senior Independent Director handles the Chair succession process, the Chair has to take the lead, working together with the board, on CEO succession.

Discussing CEO succession, one highly experienced Chair said: 'The CEO is often unlikely to choose the timing of their departure.' CEO succession has to be managed delicately, as many Chairs have said at events and in conversations for this book. Speaking at a closed-door event, one Chair said it is the CEO's time to go when they cease to be 'restless for improvement'. CEO succession should be part of the strategic discussions, not just something the Nomination Committee does, and be in service to delivering the strategy.

> 'Early-stage tech companies have investor boards and they do not want Chairs. It is founder CEOs who want a Chair – for advice, to serve as sounding board such as on hiring, and to serve as buffer between CEO and investor boards with very different priorities. VC or PE investors are answerable to their own investment committees. Mediating between people become the Chair's main job.'
>
> Chair of a tech start-up

The Chair–CEO relationship

The Chair–CEO relationship is often cited as the most critical relationship in an organization. While the CEO does not often formally participate in the Chair selection process, the CEO does need to say what they want from the Chair, and a meeting between the Chair and the CEO is often a critical component of the process.

Described as a 'three-dimensional relationship' by one Chair, the relationship can also be the most contentious. Finding the next CEO is one of the board's key responsibilities and it almost always falls to the Chair to break the news or give the tough feedback to a CEO, who has not already seen that it is time. Needless to say, Chairs and CEOs I interviewed around the world have a lot to say about the relationship (see the box on page 77).

Sometimes a new Chair may feel the need to make their mark by firing the CEO and this means there is a need, when a new Chair gets on board, to accelerate the building of a mutually trusting relationship with the CEO. Equally, a new CEO can sometimes come in and drive a wholesale change in the executive team. The board should ask for a coherent explanation and how the decisions and their timing align with the strategy.

> 'The CEO is not the sole decider… you deliver jointly on values and purpose.'
>
> Chair of a leading engineering and industrial company

The Chair can act as a mentor, a sounding board, a critical friend, and a wise partner to the CEO, who has a lonely job. The essential components of a balanced and functioning relationship are mutual trust and respect, a shared vision, clear demarcation of boundaries between roles (i.e. the Chair runs the board and the CEO runs the company), and regular and frank communication at an agreed frequency.

In good times, the CEO takes the limelight for all successes, but in challenging times, the Chair ideally protects the CEO and the executive team and if necessary, fronts all communications.

Unfortunately, there are also flawed Chair–CEO relationships in evidence and their impact on the company and beyond is often adverse. They also set the tone for the company as a whole. Speaking at London Business School, Robert Swannell CBE, Senior Adviser at Citigroup and former Chair of UK Government Investments and Marks & Spencer, described Chair–CEO dysfunction as a 'culture red flag'.[51]

While a dysfunctional Chair–CEO relationship can inflict its brand of damage, a too-close, almost co-dependent relationship can derail any chance of good governance too. In such cases the board has to get involved, usually with the Senior Independent Director or Lead Independent Director taking the lead.

One real-life experience shared in interviews was that of the CEO of a medium-sized listed company, which had been very successful in its space. The market expected the Chair to go after serving almost 10 years. Worried about Chair succession, the CEO wanted to retain the Chair in some capacity in the business, perhaps as an adviser to the CEO.

Who would raise a challenge in such a situation since it seemed here the Chair was more than keen to stay on as an adviser? The board, of course.

What would they ask? Natural questions would be: the outgoing Chair had led well for the previous 10 years, but how would he remain relevant to the next 10 years, to the business of the future? How would the former Chair be eased out with respect, if they prove not to be relevant or if they become disruptive? At any rate, how would a new Chair feel about the old Chair still hanging around the company?

Views on the Chair–CEO relationship

'Non-executive board directors need to think long-term about the future of the company, not short-term about their own reputations and fees.'

Former CEO of a FTSE 100 company

'Every board director should have access to the CEO. For open, free dialogue and for sharing information beyond meetings. But the Chair–CEO role division needs clarity. It helps their relationship.'

CEO in Italy and the USA, with experience of leading global growth for family businesses

'The Chair–CEO relationship is key and in my view, the CEO should drive it. But the Chair's skin in the game plays a role. A Chair with zero shares is unhelpful as not truly a stakeholder; on the other hand, a Chair with too large a shareholding is also counter-productive.'

CEO in the competitive hospitality sector, privately owned, in the UK

'The key success factor in a good Chair–CEO relationship is trust and mutuality. The Chair is the hidden CEO of the company in a way, directing the strategy. The CEO takes the job without knowing the reality… There is a continuum from weak CEO to strong CEO, weak Chair to strong Chair. When both are strong, there are clashes, and the Chair and the board then change the CEO. A CEO friend of mine discovered his Chair really wanted to be CEO. The Chair's ambition caused many battles. That said, a CEO will listen to an experienced Chair who picks a strong CEO, helps build the team, agrees on right outcomes, aligns strategy, and monitors the executive team.'

Four-time CEO in France, India, Austria, and Germany

'If Chair and CEO do not know how to run a board, set the agenda, and provide the right papers it creates a problem. (As CEO) my board was not valuable, they were highly perfunctory, dominant and a waste of time doing governance for the sake of it. (As founder-CEO) I had a good relationship with the board Chair, we worked through thorny issues, and the Chair advocated for me. In a founder-Chair relationship the Chair has to advocate for the founder-CEO. In lockstep. But this led to (the CEO) falling out with other board members. The Chair quit due to disgruntled board directors. The board then overturned my decisions. I felt violated, mistreated, disrespected. If a board is not engaged, it can cause harm. (As CEO of UHNW family-owned business) it is fascinating whole other dynamic. Not held to the same metrics.'

Multiple-time CEO in different ownership structures in the USA

'The Chair–CEO bromance in our company eventually killed the business. They would spend two to four hours every day on the phone, discussing things the rest of us in the exec team or the board never heard about. There was zero support for building the commercial success the business needed. There was zero accountability from the CEO. Most days he was not even showing up at work. I picked up more and more of the slack doing his job, my job, and then some. The CEO took off for his summer holiday, non-negotiable he said, while we stared at a four-month runaway and redundancies. Of course I did the redundancies over summer. It was gut-wrenching and infuriating. The Chair buckled when he should have intervened, raised a challenge to the CEO. All those long phone calls, for what?'

Former COO of a tech scale-up that had to be wound up

Questions to consider

How does work get done in this board?

What is the balance of the board's attention? Is it static or dynamic?

Balance of time spent on strategic topics and on governance/compliance topics?

Balance of board pack content between informing, discussing, ratifying, or approving?

How often does the board check the relevance or fitness-for-purpose of its makeup, agenda, and approach?

Case study: how serious boards actually work

Harmony Energy Income Trust

In the summer of 2021, I was approached to consider serving on the board of an investment company which was to be formed to raise money to procure a portfolio of shovel-ready grid-scale two-hour battery energy storage systems (BESS) projects in the UK. The projects were being developed by Harmony Energy, a Yorkshire-based developer with a track record of building BESS projects, having built Contego and Holes Bay; these were already operating.

The equity investment was to be raised via an initial public offering (IPO) on the London Stock Exchange in the Specialist Funds Segment. The company was named Harmony Energy Income Trust (stock symbol: HEIT).

A little context.

BESS has a critical role in helping countries transition to renewable energy such as solar or wind – or indeed support their net zero commitments. Solar and wind energy by their nature are intermittent – or colloquially, sometimes the sun shines, sometimes it doesn't, sometimes the wind blows, sometimes it doesn't. But when you and I want to turn the kettle on to make a cup of tea, we expect that the electricity will flow through the plug. In other words, consumers of electricity do not expect to be told that there is no power today because, well, sorry, it is cloudy. BESS is where excess energy from wind and solar power generators is stored till the grid needs it, and then the batteries discharge the stored power into the grid.

The UK has ambitious net zero goals. Grid-scale BESS is critical to reaching them. Unlike solar and wind projects though, there are no revenue guarantees, as at the time of writing in summer 2025, on offer to the BESS sector in the UK.

Back to the summer of 2021.

The putative board was constructed thoughtfully – bringing deep expertise, experience, and institutional understanding in the electricity and energy sectors, investment, technology, policy, and listed company governance, as well as a range of personalities, engagement styles, education, and social backgrounds. (Fun fact: at the time this was my third board with two directors with PhDs.)

Before deciding to join, I spoke with the asset management team as well as several others I knew in the real assets and energy storage spaces. The asset class was new and as can be expected of any new technology, there was not much historical data on revenues; at any rate the National Grid was continuing to shape the market dynamics. It shaped my ingoing view that this experience was likely to be the best and the worst of a start-up/scale-up and of a listed company. Throughout this book there are stories that highlight the differences between the boards of those two types of companies. In HEIT I feel we were fortunate to have a board with the depth of character and experience this duality of the business would demand of us.

The summer of 2021 was spent with the future directors, asset managers, and advisers working on the Prospectus. This, to the uninitiated, is an intense, time-consuming exercise requiring diligence, a lot of critical reading, verification of claims, debating and agreeing on the wording, and directors personally making guarantees. It may be worth flagging that during this time, the directors had not been appointed and were working unpaid. We were formally appointed to the board in October 2021, just a few days before the IPO.

The IPO on 9 November 2021 raised £210 million and helped acquire five shovel-ready BESS projects totalling 213.5 megawatts (MW). The company had exclusivity via a right of first refusal (ROFR) over a total of 1 gigawatts (GW) of BESS projects. The Harmony Energy projects team got to work.

So far so good.

Geopolitics strikes!

On 24 February 2022, Russia launched a military assault on Ukraine. Europe and the UK were quite reliant on Russian gas and on the day the assault began, European gas prices surged by 50% day-on-day to US$44/ Million British Thermal Units (MMBtu).[52] Asian liquified natural gas (LNG) futures rose too. This may have been good news for a company with operating BESS projects but we were not there yet. We were still building our projects and had a pipeline of projects that could be acquired.

A period of destabilization and volatility in global markets followed the launch of this war.

In the middle of all this, a debt facility was arranged in June 2022 to enable the acquisition of another, 99 MW BESS project, which was the company's first pipeline project.

The adverse macroeconomic environment however was about to ratchet pressure once again.

In the summer, we made a decision to do a capital raise to fund the acquisition and build-out of the next three BESS projects totalling 182 MW.

Domestic politics and global macroeconomics

This process rapidly got caught in the whirlwind of the change in the UK's political leadership. Liz Truss became Prime Minister for 49 days over September and October 2022. A mini-budget followed on 23 September 2022 with £45 billion of unfunded tax cuts. That catalysed several days of market turmoil, a fall in the value of the pound, and increases in UK government borrowing cost and mortgage rates.

On 12 October 2022, the Commons Treasury Committee heard from several economists where Deutsche Bank's chief UK economist Sanjay Raja characterized the mini-budget as the 'idiosyncratic UK-specific component' which alongside the already existing global turmoil served as the 'straw that broke the camel's back'.[53] That was also the day where we announced the issuance of C-shares[54] following the earlier market announcement of the intent.[55]

The HEIT board and the Harmony team held their nerve, continuing to build the existing portfolio and acquiring three projects – Wormald Green, Hawthorn Pit, and Rye Common – with the proceeds of the C-share issuance, which were lower than expected due to the turmoil.

Amid all this upheaval there was also good news. In November 2022, Pillswood, located in Cottingham in Yorkshire, was energized,[56] being 'Europe's biggest battery energy storage system' project at the time.

The year 2023 was to be mixed but it began on a positive note. We made a portfolio update after December 2022. The favourable environment for energy benefited Pillswood which outperformed all other GB BESS assets. C-shares issued earlier were converted to ordinary shares and admitted to trading.[57] Following our first full year of operating, we published our first annual results and accounts. Harmony Energy was getting some great press too.[58]

By February 2023, HEIT had seven projects under construction, with target commercial operations expected to start between Q1 2023 and Q2 2024. The company also secured contracts for Pillswood, Broadditch, Farnham, and Rusholme at the T-1 capacity market auction.[59] While the auction's clearing price of £60/megawatt hour (MWh) was slightly lower than the previous year's £75/MWh, it was still the second-highest clearing price ever achieved and higher than our current T-1 revenue assumptions. The existing debt facility was also restructured and extended to fund construction milestones, though one project, Rye Common, remained unfunded.[60]

Pillswood was formally launched on 1 March 2023 and many of our shareholders – present and prospective – attended on a bracing day in Yorkshire, giving the HEIT board and the Harmony team a moment of celebration.

Soon after, the consultation outcome[61] from the government's review of electricity market arrangements (REMA) was published by the Department of Energy Security and Net Zero (DESNZ). Respondents included investors and developers, and both groups expected REMA to deliver long-term clarity and certainty in order to retain investor confidence. They also cautioned against creating barriers to entry such as through complex market redesign.

Market jitters continued. A leading clean energy and technology group requested their shares to be temporarily suspended.[62] This was not likely to help investor nerves and was expected to increase investor scrutiny of pre-construction assets and cost increases. The interest rate environment was also encouraging investors to continue looking at alternative asset classes such as bonds and gilts, which were offering attractive yields with lower risk profiles.

BAU continued too. Pillswood 2 started to participate in the Balancing Mechanism market full-time from mid-May and Farnham was energized early in June.[63]

Internally the board got access to Harmonise, Harmony's in-house revenue and data platform, which was very helpful in seeing early trends in a new asset class with many complexities with the grid and the functioning of the market. And in August 2023, we made our first UN Principles for Responsible Investment (PRI) submission which was of special interest to me as the chair of the Environmental, Social, and Governance (ESG) committee.

At the start of autumn, BP was appointed the revenue optimizer for the Wormald Green and Hawthorn Pit projects.[64] With alternative funding avenues remaining closed, the third project acquired following the C-share issuance – Rye Common – was sold at a premium to its carrying value to Pulse Clean Energy Limited.[65]

An interesting market development followed as KKR, the New York-listed buyout giant, acquired joint control of Zenobe, one of Britain's most promising battery storage companies.[66] It was seen overall as a reassuring signal of the value of British BESS and renewables assets.

Rishi Sunak, the then-PM of the UK, delivered a net zero speech on 20 September 2023; it was widely seen as the watering down of the UK's net zero commitment even though he promised policy changes, stressed that international 2050 climate targets would still be met, committed funding for an innovation-led approach to addressing climate change, and promised a special plan for electricity infrastructure to speed up the planning process for grid connections.[67] This was once again not comforting to investors.

Amidst all this, our projects continued to receive industry recognition with Pillswood winning 'Grid-scale Standalone Energy Storage Project of the Year' at the Energy Storage Awards,[68] 'Utility Scale Storage Project of the Year' at the Solar & Storage Live Awards, and 'Best Renewable Energy Project in the Humber Area' at the Humber Renewables Awards.

The board reiterated its confidence in the company through buying further shares.

Investment Trust sector nerves

By November 2023, the London market was seeing further undesirable developments. Discounts on investment trusts were at their widest for over 15 years. Both private clients and wealth managers were selling down with seemingly only arbitrageurs buying up, and their aim was to wind down companies. Word on the street was that this was the worst market the Investment Trust sector had seen in 30 years. Certainly not an environment in which any funding could be raised.

In February 2024, alongside the annual results of the previous financial year ended October 2023, we informed the market that we had refinanced our debt[69] where the new structure reflected the evolving nature of the portfolio from under-construction to operational.

A strategic inflexion point

Challenges however continued. We had been trading at a significant discount to net asset value (NAV). Larger companies in the broader renewables sector were also trading at considerable discounts, despite their strong performances. The investment trust and real assets sectors had been experiencing outflows as interest rate increases continued to keep gilts and bonds relatively more attractive. The board was realistic about the difficulties of raising any cash if this environment persisted. We were however confident of the quality of our assets and that we could sell them at a price higher than the acquisition price.

After a review of options, we appointed Jones Lang LaSalle (JLL) to solicit offers for one, some, or all of our assets. A single asset sale would help us demonstrate the NAV, which could potentially enable raising further funds. However the board had to keep an open mind. The proceeds from any sales were set to be used to pay down debt and potentially fund share buybacks.[70] This was May 2024.

Over the next few months JLL ran a confidential process during which several interested parties conducted their due diligence. While we were heartened by the level of interest and responses in the form of non-binding offers, our main focus now was to maximize returns for our shareholders. In October we invited several bidders to a second phase.

The bid

Following further evaluation of the offers on the table, on 19 December 2024, we agreed to negotiate with a preferred bidder on an exclusive basis to sell the company's full portfolio of assets.[71] The bidder's offer was for the holding company (HoldCo), not the listed entity (PLC), so neither the bid price nor the bidder's name needed to be disclosed to the market. A further round of extensive due diligence commenced.

The exclusivity was due to expire on 12 February 2025, at which point the bidder requested an extension to 10 March 2025.[72] Even though the board was keen to complete the deal at the earliest, and was also concerned about the signal such an extension may send to the market, we agreed, as our focus remained on shareholder value and on ensuring that the deal did not get derailed.

Meanwhile our entire portfolio of projects was now fully operational. The revenue for the period November 2024 to January 2025 was found to be very pleasing.[73] The performance was owed to several factors – first, wholesale gas prices trending upwards, volatile temperatures, and stormy weather conditions created favourable circumstances; second, market conditions, which were a combination of rising wholesale price spreads and high levels of dispatch in the balancing mechanism, favoured 2h BESS. The wholesale price spreads themselves were driven by periods of low wind generation, cold weather, and higher national demand. And finally the introduction of the Quick Reserve service product – used to balance quickly energy supply and demand to keep the electrical frequency stable – by the National Energy System Operator (NESO) at the start of December 2024 also brought revenue from reserve services.

While the due diligence was underway, the board was working on our annual report and accounts, as it was uncertain that the deal would complete before the last date allowable for publishing the annual results.

Looking back now, it feels the cinema reel sped up from here on.

A new bidder

While the exclusive bidder was completing the due diligence for HoldCo, a new bidder – Foresight – made an approach. This was for the PLC. The board was alert to our responsibilities under the takeover code. The approach immediately required the board to rearrange everything else we were doing and get to work.

Foresight's proposed cash offer of 84p was at a 76% premium to the closing share price on the last business day before we had made the original announcement about the asset sale in May 2024. A PLC deal was also a 'cleaner' deal as it would not incur the winding down and delisting costs the HoldCo deal would have required.

The board gave the offer extensive consideration, a robust discussion was had, and a decision was made. We announced Foresight's offer to the market at 7am on Monday, 17 March 2025.[74]

Then a counter-offer came in – from Drax. This offer of 88p was at a premium to the Foresight bid price and also an 84% premium to the closing share price on the last business day before the asset sale announcement in May 2024. Seeking the best shareholder value being our core focus, we once again assembled, debated, and decided to accept the offer. The agreement was announced to the market on 25 March 2025.[75] Further, on 15 April 2025 the relevant acquisition scheme documentation was published, with the board's recommendation that shareholders vote in favour.

And then another counter-offer. Foresight's new offer of 92.4p now was 5% above Drax's last price and a 94% premium to the closing share price on the last business day before the asset sale announcement in May 2024. This was also at no discount to our last NAV and a substantial implied valuation of £845,000 per megawatt.

This was announced to the market on 16 April 2025.[76] The market response reflecting in our share price was enthusiastic. It also suggested that in the 2h BESS asset class, the deal was being seen as the price discovery mechanism for operational assets.

Throughout this process, the board had to understand the applicable sections of the takeover code, review detailed documentation, discuss things with advisers, make decisions, and sign off announcements. Extensive shareholder communications were sent out. Form 8.3 disclosures under the takeover code were being made pretty much every day during this time and the board kept an eye on the shareholder register, which saw several changes as the bidding war continued.[77]

An auction?

As neither of the two parties – Foresight and Drax – had declared their offer final, the Takeover Panel[78] deemed that for the purposes of Rule 32.5 of the takeover code, a competitive situation continued to exist as of 16 May 2025. At the request of both parties, the Panel Executive established an auction procedure. The auction was due to take place on the evening of 21 May 2025.[79] It is worth a mention that the use of an auction procedure is not a frequently used tool and its last use was in 2021 during the competitive takeover of Wm Morrison Supermarkets PLC in the UK.

The directors cleared their commitments for the evening of the proposed auction and were on standby; the auction normally proceeds to five rounds and may not have ended before 9pm. The board could only work on the market announcement after that. This wouldn't be the first time we had worked late into the night for a 7am market announcement the following day.

In a final development, on the evening of 20 May, Drax declared their offer of 88p final. The auction was cancelled and subject to shareholder vote, Foresight was deemed the winning bidder for HEIT PLC.

Shareholders voted for the acquisition at the general meeting on 30 May 2025. Following court proceedings, the scheme of arrangement became effective on 17 June 2025,[80] and shares were cancelled from trading on 18 June 2025.[81]

This brought the HEIT story to a dénouement, from the IPO to the acquisition and subsequent delisting, over a period of just under four years if we count the summer of 2021 spent working on the IPO preparation.

An analyst writes...

In May 2024, an analyst note compared the governance approach of the HEIT board with that of the board of another investment company owning BESS assets.[82] Drawing out the differences in engagement styles, the note said: 'The approach taken by Harmony Energy does allow them greater scope to verify, corroborate and ultimately scrutinize the manager. This becomes quite clear as they are able to discuss and debate the variety of opinions that are reflected by stakeholders in the sector.'

The note also recommended that the HEIT board should raise its fee.

Reflection

Anticipating the unanticipated. Adapting rapidly. Availability at all hours. That is pretty much the summary of how I experienced serving on the HEIT board.

In sharing this story, I have focused on the strategic decisions the HEIT board had to make, with geopolitical and macroeconomic headwinds and navigating the challenges of all our BESS assets being able to participate successfully in all the revenue streams possible given known difficulties at the National Grid. All these inflexion points and decisions were reported to the market.

Alongside the asset sale activity, which finally led to the acquisition by Foresight, we continued with the BAU – making market updates on revenue and NAV, publishing our half yearly and annual report and accounts, keeping our commitments under the United Nations Principles for Responsible Investment (UNPRI) and the Task Force on Climate-Related Financial Disclosures/Taskforce on Nature-Related Financial Disclosures (TCFD/TNFD), winning awards for our projects and for ESG communications.

BESS as an asset class is relatively new. As I mentioned earlier, this board was constructed carefully. Our approach to ensuring high-quality oversight was served not only by the cognitive diversity around the table but also by our assiduous diligence in understanding the market dynamics, engaging with stakeholders including the providers of revenue curves and other data, and close scrutiny of revenues on an asset-by-asset basis using the data dashboard to which the board had access. We deemed it necessary, especially in a low-revenue and volatile environment.

As I had anticipated – this experience, from IPO to acquisition, did turn out to be an unusual mix of founder grit and listed company compliance, a strong project builder team and a strong board, and a lot of relentless and diligent work that culminated in a decent outcome for shareholders despite odds stacked high against the business all through its existence as a listed company. The best and the worst of a start-up/scale-up and of a listed company in a volatile and mostly adversarial macroeconomic environment indeed!

(I am grateful to my HEIT board colleagues for allowing me to share this story as a way to demonstrate how sincere boards really work, and to the Harmony team and our advisers at Panmure Liberum, Gowlings, Stifel, and Berenberg for being key players in this story.)

उद्यमेन हि सिध्यन्ति कार्याणि न मनोरथैः ।
न हि सुप्तस्य सिंहस्य प्रविशंति मुखे मृगाः ॥ 36 ॥

A goal or a task is accomplished through enterprise and effort; a deer does not enter the mouth of a sleeping lion. (*Hitopadeśa* 36)

The following chapters address the trifecta of macro challenges in the current business environment – technology, climate risk, geopolitics – framing the conversation for boards considering the strategic opportunities, while foreseeing and managing risks arising from them and their interplay.

4

You and the algorithm

Connected technology now so underpins everything that to call something 'digital' is unnecessary. Own shares in a listed company? Shares are held in a dematerialized form, i.e. no paper; traded electronically, i.e. no paper; money movement to buy or from selling is by bank transfer, i.e. no paper. Teaching and tutoring students in pandemic lockdowns? All online. Operating a grid-scale battery energy storage system, connected to the electricity grid? The optimizer software plays a role in accessing the energy markets, operating to maximize revenue opportunities, and generating reports for management or boards.

Marketing your products and services to existing and potential customer base? Outdoor, print, broadcast media, direct mailers, and product placements now co-exist with digital marketing which includes online ads, native advertising, interstitials in subscription products and apps, social media, in-product advertising, and sponsorships of digital product formats. Formats such as QR codes use a physical asset, e.g. a print ad, to nudge the reader to scan the code to access a digital property such as a website. The proverbial wasted half of the advertising money can now be tracked more assiduously and allocations of messaging and media can be modified in near-real time too.

With suppliers, customers, and employees all connected to the company's systems, data is constantly coming in, going out, being accessed, being stored, and being processed for a range of purposes. These include producing business intelligence, supporting compliance and reporting, implementing predictive and Generative AI systems, and enabling innovation. Every exchange of data could be a point where malicious action could compromise the systems.

Digital has supplanted physical in many situations, while creating audit trails in real time. With everything connected, the risk of cyber attacks is higher than ever. This issue demands attention as cyber criminals professionalize and become better organized, encouraged by the absence of any agreed global frameworks for prosecuting cross-border crimes. The question of jurisdiction aside, investigating and prosecuting these crimes demands much coordination; Interpol and Europol are but coordination efforts, not enforcement mechanisms, for which countries' own law enforcement structures come into play.

All of this requires board scrutiny. That scrutiny needs to keep up with emerging changes as well as new issues that arise – and that is an uncharted space. As much as one makes progress in that space, one encounters and has to deal with the wilderness.

> Boards of companies are therefore understandably keen to have 'technology' talent.

With rapid changes in the technology space, it may be less important to have someone who ran a large transformation 15 years ago than to have someone whose finger is on the pulse through continuing engagement with emerging technologies today – an idea that is a tough sell to boards, especially those that may not be very tech-fluent.

How are boards to evaluate someone's technology knowledge? Will that person become the board's 'tech whisperer' if the rest of the board is not keeping up? Can one person be scrutinizing infrastructure, cyber, data, and AI? If not one person, how many technology 'experts' can the board accommodate? Where is the technology polyglot and how will the board evaluate their thinking?

> The only way forward is for all directors to stay abreast of things tech while evaluating them from the lens of the work of stewardship. Stewardship needs more than 'tech', it needs the ability to ask questions that evolve and morph with tech.

Time horizon for strategic thinking

Apple first debuted its dedicated neural network hardware in September 2017, with its A11 Bionic chip used in the iPhone 8.[1] The process of designing its own silicon took almost 10 years before that.[2] The first Apple-designed system-on-a-chip (SoC) was launched in 2010[3] and Apple fully switched to its own chips in 2020. Apple launched its software AI – Apple Intelligence – which uses on-device and server processing in June 2024.[4]

Apple designed its SoC and system in a package (SiP) processors using ARM architecture. ARM architecture was designed by Acorn Computers, a British technology company that spun-off its architecture business under a joint venture with Apple and VLSI in 1990.[5]

Zen Robotics, a company founded in 2007 to recycle waste, has built deep understanding of waste separation and recycling. Since launching their first robots in 2009 for waste separation and sorting, the company claims that its robots can now handle over 350 waste fractions – fraction being the term for waste classification – including construction and demolition waste, commercial waste, packaging waste, scrap metals, rigid plastics, wood waste, municipal solid waste, and mixed recycling.[6] The AI underlying the robots has been trained on these waste fractions and can operate with precision without needing much human oversight. This use of hardware AI serves the need for circularity in materials and for sorting waste efficiently. By 2021 the company had launched many industrial material recovery facilities globally.

Whether one looks at the time from the Apple–VLSI joint venture to the SoC launch, or the time between the debut of the neural network hardware and the launch of Apple Intelligence, these are some pretty long time horizons for Apple's successes to have incubated. The Zen Robotics story too unfolds over a long period of time.

As stewards of a company's long-term success, we need to consider: what does 'long-term' mean? What is the time horizon for strategic investments and for calculating return on investment? How often are the assumptions reviewed? Long strategic thinking horizons naturally demand patience and commitment but also a clear-eyed view of the strategic impact, and the ability to communicate clearly to shareholders and markets in order to retain their support.

> There is an element of selfless service in stewardship. Strategically meaningful things may come to fruition way past our term on the board. There will be no credit given to us for those successes, while failures and oversights may well be attributed to us. This is a personal risk assessment all aspiring board directors may wish to undertake for themselves.

New risks, new rails

Contrast these long strategic horizons with the urgency, even FOMO, being felt by boards and business leaders when it comes to Generative AI. Microsoft CoPilot reminding us of 'Clippy, but in a collared shirt' seems positively tame compared to other challenges that can bring serious consequences.

In mid-2023, a New York judge fined two lawyers who submitted fake cases generated by ChatGPT to support their claim; the judge said the lawyers had 'abandoned their responsibilities when they submitted non-existent judicial opinions with fake quotes and citations created by the artificial intelligence tool ChatGPT, then continued to stand by the fake opinions after judicial orders called their existence into question'. It 'promotes cynicism' about judicial precedent, the judge said.[7]

In June 2025, in a stern intervention, judge Victoria Sharp, president of the King's Bench Division of the High Court of England and Wales, issued a formal warning to legal professionals, declaring that lawyers who submit fictitious cases generated by artificial intelligence could face contempt proceedings or referral to their regulator.[8] She noted that misuse of artificial intelligence could create 'serious implications for the administration of justice and public confidence in the justice system'.

Law is but one of the highly regulated sectors where there are considerable second- and third-order consequences. The risks therefore cascade. How do boards in these sectors articulate and evaluate cascading risks? What guardrails are required? How do accountability and oversight work?

> Boards of companies in regulated sectors, where business decisions have second- and third-order consequences, need to bring extra vigilance to emerging technologies and the cascading risks posed by them to balance with the opportunities presented by the same technologies.

Starting with the end in mind

Technology can also be used to manage and mitigate risk, and enable great outcomes. Africa Prize 2025 winner Margaret Wanjiku, as a child in rural Kenya, learnt the role of bees in pollination and agriculture.[9] Growing up, she saw the problem of beehive collapse which threatens food security and ecosystems. Along with a team, Margaret designed a small Internet of Things (IoT)-device called Smart Hive for real-time monitoring of hive conditions. Installed at the base of a beehive, it tracks temperature, humidity, and hive activity. The system processes this data, combines with AI analytics, and sends text updates to beekeepers, so they can take action to protect their beehives. To ensure beekeepers even in remote areas can monitor their hives, Smart Hive draws power from a built-in solar panel, removing the reliance on external electricity sources.

Her company also supports small-scale farmers with precision pollination services. Satellite imagery and advanced mapping are used to determine strategic placement for beehives based on crop type, bloom schedules, and weather patterns, to maximize pollination.

Kalyani Shinde, a young engineering student in India and daughter of an onion farmer, grew up in Asia's largest onion trading town.[10] She was aware of up to 800% fluctuations in the price of onions. Onions take about 120 days from sowing to harvesting, and are stored for six to eight months. Farmers usually rely on smells in the warehouse to detect spoilage and can lose 30–50% of their stored crop. In 2018 Kalyani started by assessing warehouses for their air flow, ventilation, and floor spacing to maintain a desirable 30% water content in onions and built an IoT solution to detect gases emitted by spoilt onions in warehouses, to collect real-time data, and to alert the farmers.

While she sells directly to farmers, she also collaborates with larger businesses to build better warehouses, complete with solar panels. Her solution is shown to reduce wastage by 20–25%.

It may be tempting to conclude from these stories that such new solutions can only be found for entirely new problems discovered in virgin environments. That would be inaccurate.

New York City in the USA has a comprehensive IoT strategy.[11] A foundational report in 2015 was followed by wide-ranging stakeholder consultation including public sector, private sector, academia, and government agencies across the world, which helped identify 450 best practices for IoT. Pilot projects began in 2018. Several key projects such as BigBelly smart bins, to make waste collection more efficient, and smart water meters to prevent water wastage, are helping the city become less wasteful and more responsive.

In adopting Generative AI – or any other innovative technology such as AI-optimized IoT, as in the examples above – it always helps to start with identifying problems that need solving. And then consider: what desirable outcomes are envisaged? What resource assumptions are being made in designing the solution? What additional risks come into play and how can they be mitigated?

> In considering an innovative technology, it helps to start by identifying the problems that may be amenable to being solved with that technology. Problem-first, not technology-first framing may help unlock new opportunities.

Move fast, don't break things

In 2022, Air Canada's customer support chatbot gave incorrect information to a customer. The customer was assured that he could book a full-fare flight for a family funeral and apply for a bereavement fare after the fact. When the customer followed the advice, the airline refused to extend the discount, suggesting that the customer should have read the policy on the link provided by the chatbot. In court, the airline argued its chatbot is 'responsible for its own actions', lost the case, and was asked to pay damages and tribunal fees.[12]

In 2025, Delta Airlines has said that they intend to roll out 'AI based pricing' to 20% of its fares.[13] The AI tool would set prices and determine how many seats are on offer at that price in a sort of 'offer management' system. Swift backlash followed, and a Senator warned against 'surveillance pricing',[14] forcing Delta to issue a denial and an explanation of how it may use AI for offering fares.[15] It is hard to see how any of this may have been brand equity-enhancing for Delta.

> When a business is moving fast to implement rapidly evolving tech, such as chatbots, into its customer-facing processes, board oversight may require asking about additional control and accountability mechanisms and their fitness for purpose. Customer-facing processes should not become customer-failing processes.

Living on the edge (AI)

The 'extremely online' already know that Maslow's hierarchy has had an update. It adds two layers below physiological needs. Right below this layer is 'wi-fi' and the new foundation layer is 'battery'. Jokes apart, this encapsulates a fundamental truth of life as a connected ecosystem of businesses, suppliers, and consumers: it needs power and consumes rather a lot of it. Hence the vital role of electricity grids in the connected world.

Renewable energy sources, like solar and wind, and grid-scale battery energy storage systems, are being integrated into the grids. Grids need to be more resilient. Here is where edge AI has... an edge, beyond smart meters and sensors. Smart edge devices with processing power can perform complex calculations; run protection, fault isolation, and service restoration algorithms; and make autonomous decisions about specific grid functions, such as managing quality, load balancing, voltage optimization etc.[16]

Not all edge AI needs complex new hardware. High mobile penetration and use in vast expanses of the African continent and the Indian subcontinent enable bringing edge AI without much fuss – improving the lives of farmers and bringing healthcare to low-resource devices in remote areas. In rural areas in several states in India, Swasth AI serves as a healthcare assistant to auxiliary nurse midwives, accredited social health activists, and rural doctors;[17] it helps amongst other things with risk detection such as in high-risk pregnancies, and offline access to medical guidelines to improve maternal and child health and rural healthcare. It also supports regional languages and voice-based care for non-literate users. Critically, it works without internet access. In Zimbabwe, a WhatsApp-based chatbot called Nyamukuta is delivering pre- and post-pregnancy care; WhatsApp works even in low bandwidth or slow web access areas, thus overcoming not only technical but also sociological challenges such as the danger of travelling in remote areas.[18]

The battery management on your laptop or your phone too is an example of edge AI. As is your web-connected smart car – with its safety features such as lane departure warnings, collision detection, automatic emergency braking, and intelligent navigation features using real-time traffic data.

By enabling computing tasks to be performed closer to data sources, edge AI helps reduce latency. It can be a superior way to implement automation, improve decision-making, and indeed create innovative solutions either for our business processes or for our customers.

Not without risks though.

Edge AI opens a wider attack surface. Without robust end-point security, strong encryption, authentication, and firmware protection, every edge device can potentially compromise entire networks. For instance, routers account for 75% of all IoT infections.[19] Increased data sharing creates a data security risk – for privacy, potential for data breaches, and compliance challenges at scale. Model theft, model extraction, and reverse engineering remain risks to AI models deployed at the edge. Besides IP compromise, the models can be put to malicious use. In a hyper-distributed environment, complex model updates can be quite challenging.

> Edge AI is increasingly cost-effective and a faster way to implement AI solutions. Managing the additional risks due to a larger attack surface requires imagination to anticipate and mitigate.

AI could give your brand a bad name

Apologies are owed to Bon Jovi who was singing about something else. In 2023, an article about a London Stock Exchange listed company, with a negative, click-bait headline, appeared near the top in the Apple News section in the Apple Stocks app.[20] On clicking through, the article noted the positives in the company and its strong trading position compared to peers. But the longer note to drill down further was paywalled.

The staccato tone suggested it may have been machine-written. Or AI slop, as we call it now.

There was nothing the marketing team could do about the misleading headline. There was no appeal mechanism and the company had to wait several weeks for further press coverage to push the misleading article down the list of articles appearing on the Stocks app.

Indeed, Generative AI is enabling other kinds of mischief – deepfakes. While women online have long been familiar with the risk of their likeness being misused to create revenge videos and malicious content, CFOs and CEOs are discovering the risks now – although voice cloning-based scams were already happening as far back as 2019.[21]

British engineering firm Arup lost US$25 million when a deepfake fraud was visited on the company in Hong Kong.[22] A senior manager was digitally cloned and a financial transfer ordered in a video conference call. The CEO of advertising firm WPP was also the target of a deepfake scam; criminals cloned his voice and used public YouTube footage to set up a video conference with his executive team with the pretext of setting up a new business, eventually asking for personal details and money.[23]

Denmark is one of the first-mover states in legal attempts to protect individual digital identity.[24] The country is redefining copyright law to give every individual legal ownership over their own physical likeness – face, body, voice. Individuals will have the right to assert copyright in their likeness, as seen in realistic, digitally generated imitations, and demand removal and seek damages. Platforms that fail to remove deepfake content will face fines. Successful passage and operationalizing of the law could serve as a model for regulating synthetic content online.

AI slop and deepfakes are novel risks to brands, professional and personal reputations, and share prices. A brand underpins a business's trustworthiness. Social listening may or may not surface AI slop, or keep up with the pace of AI slop, or manage to control anything before damage is done. The surface area of reputational risks is so much greater with automated and synthetic content. Absent regulation of AI, these risks need constant vigilance from businesses. How can boards track and oversee risks from malicious or adversarial commentary online for which nobody can be held accountable? What realistic controls can be put in place, especially when so many parameters online are increasingly out of our control? Under pressure, how would the board respond to a potential deepfake scam being visited on any one or more of them?

In 2024, an executive at Ferrari received several WhatsApp messages that appeared to have come from the CEO, Benedetto Vigna.[25] The messages mentioned an impending acquisition, urging the executive to sign a non-disclosure agreement. Despite a profile picture of Vigna, the Ferrari logo, and the voice mimicking Vigna's accent, the executive noticed inconsistencies in a follow-up call. The executive then asked the caller a question, the answer to which only Vigna would know. He asked him the title of a book Vigna had recommended earlier. Unable to answer the question, the scammer abruptly ended the call. The executive's presence of mind and scepticism may have prevented a potential financial loss and reputational damage for Ferrari.

> AI slop and deepfakes can undermine a business in many ways but vigilance, scepticism, and interpersonal relationship detail can still work as adjuncts to controls, as the Ferrari story shows. Boards might even want to consider unannounced drills or test runs for scam calls, and review the lessons learnt.

Sovereign-sponsored AI

Switzerland announced the launch in 2025 of Apertus, a publicly developed large language model (LLM).[26] It is fully open – meaning its source code and model weights and intermediate checkpoints are publicly available, its training data is transparent and reproducible, and it is downloadable under an open licence.[27] It is available in two sizes – 8 billion and 70 billion parameters – for varying user needs, and downloadable from Swisscom or Hugging Face.

The base model was trained on 15 trillion tokens in over 1,000 languages, 40% non-English, as well as code and mathematics data, giving it multilingual fluency. It has been co-created at EPFL and ETH Zurich, joint leaders of the Swiss AI Initiative, and trained at the Swiss National Supercomputing Centre (CSCS). The model is developed in alignment with Swiss data protection laws, Swiss copyright laws, and the transparency obligations under the EU AI Act.

The Government of India's IndiaAI mission chose Sarvam, an Indian AI company, to build three sovereign models – Sarvam-Large for advanced reasoning and generation, Sarvam-Small for real-time interactive applications, and Sarvam-Edge for compact on-device tasks.[28] India is focusing on cheaper, customizable, and inclusive small language models, or SLMs, building on its tradition of frugal engineering and its digital infrastructure (described in the following section).[29]

South Korea has appointed a senior presidential secretary dedicated to AI, with an ambition to be in the global top three in AI by 2027.[30] An investment of US$735 billion is to be made into state-backed infrastructure, semiconductor dominance, and strategic partnerships, to develop sovereign AI using Korean language and data.

> Locally developed, government-sponsored sovereign AI systems are tapping into national sentiments of ambition and cultural identity and concerns about security and relevance amid geopolitical instability and uncertainty. They may catalyse firm and sustainable demand for chipmakers, data centre providers, and other key enablers of AI but may complicate the pressure that businesses already feel about Generative AI. Businesses and their boards need to remain agile and responsive to strategic challenges that may arise from the interplay of these developments.

Money, it's a gas...

Smart Hive, mentioned earlier, is an example of a distributed system architecture where the components are in different locations but working to a common goal using their collective power. Decentralized protocols take a further step towards community governance and greater resilience in systems.

Decentralized social networking protocols are emerging rapidly. User data, content moderation, network infrastructure control, and ownership are distributed across a network of nodes or participants, rather than being centralized under a single entity. Mastodon was created as a decentralized microblogging platform, but in the wake of the change in ownership of Twitter, now known as X, BlueSky gained prominence. It is an open-source client app built on top of an open protocol. Those who moved from X to BlueSky lamented the loss of their communities, but should they want to move from BlueSky, it allows them to migrate their social accounts to any other social media network using that same protocol.[31]

Beckn Protocol,[32] developed in India by a team including Nandan Nilekani, who has played a key role in the development of the India Stack (more below), is an open and interoperable protocol for decentralized digital commerce. It enables discovery of businesses and peer-to-peer interaction between businesses, service providers, and consumers. It is technology-agnostic, with a range of use cases in sectors such as digital commerce, logistics, mobility, and healthcare.

Decentralized finance, however, is perhaps the best-known use case in the business community and boardrooms, due to much discussion across the ecosystem of banks, regulators, and payment schemes over the years. JP Morgan issued their own cryptocurrency as far back as 2019, in a first for a USA bank.[33] The mainstreaming and the support of the state and regulatory apparatus are more recent.

In China, the regulator overseeing the assets of state-owned enterprises has been encouraging them to explore the role of stablecoin[34] and other digital assets in trade. In a separate development, Hong Kong passed a stablecoin bill in summer 2025, creating the region's first mandatory licensing regime for digital currencies. The law will apply to any stablecoin pegged to the HK dollar or issued locally and is in effect as of 1 August 2025. For issuers it mandates one-to-one reserve backing, a minimum capital of HK$25 million, and quarterly audits. It also grants Hong Kong authority over any foreign stablecoin promoted, marketed, or made available to the public in Hong Kong, preempting regulatory arbitrage between countries.

Hong Kong's digital asset strategy covers stablecoins and other tokenized digital products such as cryptocurrencies and central bank digital currencies. Regulations cover four 'blocks' of digital assets: exchanges, stablecoin issuers, dealing service providers, and custodians. Standard Chartered, Hong Kong Telecom, and Animoca Brands have planned to set up a joint venture to issue a Hong Kong dollar-backed stablecoin under licence from the Hong Kong Monetary Authority.[35] The stablecoin can be used for retail transactions and traded on any of the approved virtual-asset exchanges with investible assets.

Fun fact: Tether Holdings SA is the issuer of the world's largest stablecoin (USDT). Its Swiss vault reportedly contains about US$8 billion of gold, or almost 80 tons of the metal, making the stablecoin issuer one of the largest holders of gold outside of banks and nation states.[36]

In summer 2025 the USA passed the Guiding and Establishing National Innovation for U.S. Stablecoins Act (GENIUS Act) to regulate payment stablecoins. Similar to the Hong Kong law, it lays down standards for reserves, quarterly audits, and transparency for stablecoin issuers, and establishes a federal and state supervisory system to mitigate financial stability risks and protect consumers. The Act will give stablecoins the same liquidity treatment as money market funds, and gives stablecoin holders senior status over all other creditors in bankruptcy proceedings. Like the Hong Kong bill, the Act requires offshore issuers targeting USA-based users to relocate onshore within 12 months. In late summer 2025, the state of Wyoming became the first state to issue a stablecoin, named Frontier Stable Token or FRNT.[37] Flat-pegged to the US dollar, it was deployed on seven blockchains at launch.

Countries and supranational bodies are innovating in other, broader ways too. India showcased its Digital Public Infrastructure (DPI) at a G2 session in March 2023. The 'India Stack' includes a digital identification layer called Aadhar; a payments system running as a Unified Payment Interface; and a data exchange layer in its Account Aggregators.[38] These foundational layers can be used to build, iterate, and innovate upon. In early 2025, 'Euro Stack' was announced to enable a digital infrastructure built on common platforms, data spaces, standards, and coordinated strategies and investments.[39]

Decentralization and digital public infrastructure enable potentially new and creative branding opportunities. Boards need to up their game on branding. Who really 'owns' the brand? Who owns the brand message? Can different messages go to different audiences depending on where we engage with them? How to grow the brand in this new paradigm?

Financial services firms have considerable opportunity in tokenized and digital assets, though the focus perhaps should be first-principles based, on using blockchain for instance as a way to reduce costs in transaction services.

> There is collective intelligence in decentralized assets, analogous to how boards assemble a range of talents and then create value through elicitation of the tacit wisdom around the table. There is also considerable opportunity for branding and for new products and services.

***

The foregoing is not an exhaustive list of all tech-enabled disruptions and discontinuities. It is however a snapshot of possibilities and provocations that businesses face today, and that, with their rapidly evolving nature, demand or indeed enable a strategic renewal greater than tinkering on the edges of a five-year strategic plan.

- Technology's inevitable march is dissolving older, hard-and-fast boundaries between industry sectors, reshaping business models, and creating a new landscape of business risks and opportunities. The changes are flagging off the journey from governance and compliance towards true stewardship. The uncharted space can be mapped, starting with the right intentions.

5

Business in choppy waters

'Court finds no duty of care owed to Torres Strait Islanders over climate change' – this is how a headline summarized the judgement handed down by Judge Michael Wigney of Australia's Federal Court, in the (northern hemisphere) summer of 2025.[1] The court also rejected the Islanders' claims that their cultural loss should be compensated under negligence law. Similar to the early copyright violation cases brought against vendors of Generative AI (see **Chapter 6**), this case too turned on a technicality – not because there was no merit in the allegations, but because negligence law does not allow compensation for matters of government policy. The judge also noted that in setting emissions targets between 2015 and 2021 to hold global temperatures to 1.5 degrees Celsius, Australia 'did not engage with or give real or genuine consideration to the best available science'.

A few months before that, German courts rejected Peruvian farmer Saúl Luciano Lliuya's lawsuit against German energy company RWE, where he argued that the company's global emissions contributed to the melting of glaciers in Peru.[2] He sought compensation to build flood defences to protect his hometown Huaraz from the resulting flooding. While Mr Lliuya lost the case, the court said that energy companies could be held responsible for the costs caused by their carbon emissions.

In 2020, a 25-year-old member had sued the Australian superannuation fund REST Super for failing to provide information related to climate change business risks as well as any plans made to address them. REST Super settled the litigation and said that 'climate change is a material, direct and current financial risk to the superannuation fund', and that its portfolio will be aligned to reach net-zero emissions by 2050.[3] In 2024, in a case brought about by older Swiss women regarding the Swiss government's inadequate climate action, the European Court of Human Rights (ECHR) ruled that government inaction on climate change violates fundamental human rights.[4] In 2025, four Portuguese young persons filed a case against the government of Portugal with a hope to force the country to set tougher targets to cut greenhouse gas emissions and to lay out long-term plans for carbon neutrality.[5]

> Climate inaction-related litigation is one of the more visible risks that businesses and governments are facing. But these are far from the only risks to the survival, let alone long-term success of businesses, on the one planet we share.

Supply chains under pressure

In the 1980 PBS television show *Free to Choose,* Milton Friedman described the global economy using Leonard Read's essay *I, Pencil: My Family Tree as Told to Leonard E. Read*:[6]

> 'Look at this lead pencil. There is not a single person in this world who can make this pencil. Remarkable statement? Not at all.
>
> The wood from which it's made, for all I know, comes from a tree that was cut down in the State of Washington. To cut down that tree, it took a saw. To make the saw, it took steel. To make the steel, it took iron ore. This black centre, we call it lead but it's really graphite, compressed graphite, I'm not sure where it comes from, but I think it comes from some mines in South America. This red top up here, the eraser, a bit of rubber, probably comes from Malaya, where the rubber tree isn't even native. It was imported from South America by some businessmen with the help of the British government. This brass ferrule – I haven't

> the slightest idea where it came from, or the yellow paint, or the paint that made the black lines, or the glue that holds it together.
>
> Literally thousands of people cooperated to make this pencil, people who don't speak the same language, who practice different religions, who might hate one another if they ever met. When you go down to the store and buy this pencil, you are in effect, trading a few minutes of your time for a few seconds of the time of all of those thousands of people.
>
> What brought them together and induced them to cooperate to make this pencil?
>
> There was no commissar sending out offices, sending out orders from some central office. It was the magic of the price system, the impersonal operation of prices that brought them together, and got them to cooperate to make this pencil so that you could have it for a trifling sum. That is why the operation of the free market is so essential, not only to promote productive efficiency, but, even more, to foster harmony and peace among the peoples of the world.'

What might an analogous essay 'I, chocolate' or 'I, air conditioner' look like?

Mars Inc., owner of chocolate products[7] such as Snickers, M&Ms, Celebrations, Bounty, and of course the Mars Bar, appears to have given that question some thought. Cacao is an essential ingredient of those popular brands, but it faces climate variability, plant diseases, and environmental stresses. In the summer of 2025, Mars Inc. agreed to license Pairwise's Fulcrum® gene-editing tools for cacao research and development[8] to develop cacao that could be more resilient to diseases and climate. These tools use CRISPR[9] (which stands for 'clustered interspaced short palindromic repeats') to enable more precise gene-editing.

Whether we make cars or white goods, offer financing or software-as-a-service, operate in the Global North or the Global South, the exercise to unpack our business's supply chain is informative, and focuses the board's mind.

It might also be instructive to think what that unpacking might look like: moves are afoot towards deglobalization (see **Chapter 6**), decoupling supply chains, and reducing interdependence between nation states in favour of economic nationalism and new alliances; and supply chains and value chains need to decarbonize urgently. As of summer 2025, scientists warn us that we are at risk of breaching the 1.5C warming limit by 2028.[10]

The scope and scale of the changes required, for companies and countries alike, demand structural changes in economies; in business, these changes necessitate a change in how capital allocation decisions are made. We are perilously close to a disorderly climate transition, with heightened rate of economic and social change needed, at a great cost, and at greater risks. This transition risk sits alongside physical risk from exposure to extreme weather events, and other hazards such as extreme heat, water stress, and drought.

> Keeping all that in mind, the board needs to ask some questions. Who will need our products in the future? Where will we source raw materials? Could we offer new products? How can we think more creatively about our sourcing and production processes? What new alliances could we forge that we may not have considered before? Will there be a business at all? What do we need to start doing right away? How do we explain this to our shareholders?

Insurability, backstops, and nature-based solutions

The chief underwriting officer for Swiss Re, one of the world's biggest reinsurers, recently said that the insurance industry significantly underestimated the fallout from recent natural disasters across Europe and warned that some areas have become 'uninsurable', 'whether it's the

Turkey quake… or the floods in Germany or the hailstorms in Italy, models were off by factors as opposed to 10 or 20 per cent'.[11]

A paper published by The African Risk Capacity (ARC) highlights that over the last decade, the frequency of weather-related natural disasters has steadily increased in 29 African countries and estimates that African governments spent US$2.2 billion managing weather-related natural disasters in 2023.[12] The insurance protection gap however is vast in the continent. For instance, across Africa, just 7% of natural-disaster losses were covered by insurance, according to Aon's figures.

The tools to mitigate disaster risk being used in the Global South include: publicly backed schemes, either to help improve climate resilience or to share their risks; a fund being developed by the Insurance Development Forum to build 'resilient and sustainable infrastructure'; public-private schemes known as 'microinsurance'; and national-level programmes to pool the risk of big catastrophes such as hurricanes between different countries.[13]

Insurance is also helping minimize the impact of adverse events on biodiversity and eco-services. For instance, China's first Gross Ecosystem Product (GEP) insurance programme insured wetland carbon sinks at Hangzhou Bay National Wetland Park in the Ningbo region, with Swiss Re providing the risk platform.[14]

The Lloyd's Register Foundation World Risk Poll interestingly found that while southeast Asia is one of the most disaster-prone areas in the world, the people in this region have better disaster preparedness and feeling of agency than almost anywhere else. About 62% live in a household with a plan that all members of the household know in case of future disaster, and 67% feel agency in being able to protect themselves and their families.[15] The Philippines, Vietnam, and Cambodia stand out for disaster preparedness; and a majority in all southeast Asian countries received early warnings before disaster – demonstrating how resilience can be built in communities and regions at risk.

At the same time, mentions of climate change, droughts, floods, wildfires, and extreme heat in securities filings being made by businesses in the USA declined year on year 31% in the first five months of 2025, per a Wall Street Journal analysis.[16] This is despite the numerous environmental disasters within the past year, including the Los Angeles wildfires, the hurricanes in Florida, and the storms and flooding in North Carolina, and more recently, flash flooding in Texas. This may be due to the change in the political environment but is not necessarily a great development. Meanwhile in 2024, global banks' financing for coal, oil, and gas projects rose by 23%.[17]

The insurance industry is innovating variously, e.g. regional reinsurance pools, often backed by governments; resilience bonds linking investor returns to resilience outcomes; parametric insurance or carbon credit warranties, particularly for infrastructure; and blended finance for key projects in the Global South.

Nature-based solutions offer an effective and sustainable approach, combining ecological, social, and technological knowledge, to promote mitigation as well as adaptation through enhancing the resilience of ecosystems.[18] Financing too needs to flow away from activities that harm nature towards activities that support it and help restore biodiversity and improve land degradation.

Boards need to consider the insurability of the businesses they oversee. Many businesses are now building their own risk maps and working closely with insurers to build preemptive and proactive measures into their infrastructure, buildings, and manufacturing plants. Those who oversee multicountry operations will need to rethink their framing of climate risk and the cost of not addressing it.

Water and waste

Over the last 20 years, Coca-Cola in India has been accused of several poor business practices: over-extraction of ground water has left water-scarce regions in Rajasthan[19] and Uttar Pradesh with dramatic drops in the water tables, threatening their livelihoods; contamination of local water resources such as in Kerala,[20] through hazardous levels of cadmium and lead, leaving water toxic and unfit for agricultural or domestic use, in addition to creating health issues for the local people; and poor waste management, where the sludge from manufacturing was found to be toxic.

In 2025, data centres owned by Meta in the state of Georgia in the USA are reportedly disrupting wells and water tables, causing build-up of sediment, reducing water pressure, and making 'taps run dry'.[21]

These are two very different industries but they show a common theme: the negative externalities visited upon communities and society at large.

> Water is a basic necessity, doubly so in arid or semi-arid regions, and responsible waste management, not least for discharging extended producer responsibility obligations, needs to be on the board's agenda for climate resilience. This is relevant for businesses that sell goods as well as those that sell services.

Leapfrogging versus incumbency

Although the Global North remains the biggest contributor to climate change, climate-related risks are more prominent in the Global South, where temperature extremes, severe droughts, flooding, loss of biodiversity, water stress, and decline in food production are just some of the effects. The dependencies on the Earth are higher, including spiritual linkages, and the impact on livelihoods is direct and sizeable.

On the bright side – as put to me by the leader of the Net Zero and Decarbonization strategy of one of the world's largest corporations[22] – there is no climate change denialism in the Global South. The Global

South, she added, feels the urgency but also has the optimism, the drive, and the energy to make things better, and they are hungry to get going. The key bottleneck is financing.

The North-South divide in climate transition is essentially the story of leapfrogging versus incumbency. The Global South does not have much old infrastructure to replace; they are building anew, they are a new market so to speak for breakthrough innovations. Indeed, east Asia leads on growth of renewable energy generation.[23] The Global North on the other hand has incumbency issues, well-established lobbies, resistance to change, and a need for asset replacement, all of which need to be overcome or solved.

Nation states as well as corporations have the opportunity to lead the change, and some are taking that opportunity. In October 2023, the Monetary Authority of Singapore (MAS) set out a framework that includes guidelines for financial institutions (banks, insurers, asset managers) to improve their transition planning.[24] A US$500 million pledge to help decarbonize Asia followed in November 2024, whereby the Singapore government would provide concessional funding on favourable terms to match concessional capital from multilateral development banks, other governments, and philanthropic foundations.[25] The recognition of the criticality of sustainability taxonomy interoperability has since then resulted in MAS, the People's Bank of China (PBOC), and the European Union Directorate-General for Financial Stability, Financial Services and Capital Markets Union launching the Multi-Jurisdiction Common Ground Taxonomy;[26] and in July 2025, MAS and PBOC reaffirmed their commitment to strengthening taxonomy interoperability.[27] Singapore is recognized as the most active green finance hub in Asia.[28]

BlackRock, the world's largest asset manager, is navigating the transatlantic divide on taking public positions on climate risk.[29] It is however also working on better risk modelling to attract more capital to transition-financing in the Global South.[30]

> These differences in attitudes and opportunities mean businesses have an opportunity to reimagine their approach in the Global South, including in terms of the relevance of products and pricing, as well as, where relevant to their core business, the opportunity to think imaginatively and creatively about financing the transition.

The need for shared stories

Alex Evans has written about the need for shared myths to help us conceptualize what we are experiencing before we aim to solve it.[31] Shared stories about people, their trials and tribulations, change and transitions in history, things being broken and mended. Karen Armstrong, comparative religion scholar and writer, says further: 'A myth does not impart factual information, but is primarily a guide to behaviour. Its truth will only be revealed if it is put into practice – ritually or ethically.'[32] Carl Jung describes myths as 'the psychic life of the primitive tribe, which immediately falls into pieces and decays when it loses its mythological heritage, like a man who has lost his soul'.[33] More recently, Joan Didion reminded us how 'we tell ourselves stories in order to live'.[34]

A globally shared challenge of climate change, where leaders nonetheless continue to protect national interests and short-termism, needs a shared myth. Not of doom and gloom. But of optimism and future-readiness.

Who is telling those stories in your business?

Stories, what stories? As a board director, you might even baulk at the suggestion! But you shouldn't. Your brands tell stories that enable your customers to imagine how the brand could have a place in their lives. Stories that reject 'collapsitarianism' and 'effective accelerationism' in favour of the vision of a more meaningful future now need to be told.

The myths we need require a collectivist view, a longer view of the future, and a more purposeful vision of our future together. The debate on whose job it is to provide and share these myths is not settled, but forward-thinking boards that focus on their job of stewardship could take a bold step in taking the lead.

***

While systems change for climate action may not come overnight, it needs to be accelerated and it needs to be driven by optimism, because time horizons for action are short and shrinking. Prioritizing nature-based solutions – ecosystem restoration and conservation, sustainable management of biodiversity, and traditional knowledge about the functioning of natural systems, held within communities that are spiritually close to nature and rely on it for their livelihoods – and combining them with strategic decarbonization of energy and food systems will require commitment and leadership.

Future-relevant boards need to address the factors that hold back climate action – lack of prioritization, short-term thinking, gaps in knowledge, and lack of financial incentive.[35] They may also need to lead on shared stories that motivate and exhort collaborative action because no one person, business, or nation alone is going to solve these challenges. The urgency to address the transition brings us into an uncharted space and our relevance as the human race may well depend on our ability to make bold strides into that space.

6

Geo-sensibilities and choices

The South American nation Guyana is, in 2025, the only country in the world that produces enough food, in all seven food groups, to feed itself without any reliance on imports.[1] This is the result of a multifaceted policy supporting its agriculture sector and its arable lands. While an early pioneer of a low-carbon development strategy, the country has embraced oil and gas to become one of the fastest-growing economies in the world. Rich in natural resources, Guyana is in the process of becoming one of the world's biggest producers of offshore oil and gas, with ExxonMobil undertaking both exploration and production. The agreement with ExxonMobil is widely understood to be lopsided and here are the paradoxes.

Guyana's coastal areas and its port infrastructure face a threat from rising sea levels due to global warming. Nearly 85% of Guyana's landmass is covered in tropical rain forests that are home to the world's most biodiverse, intact, globally valuable ecosystem.[2] A 2024 study estimated that in 2025, Guyana would release 11,015 kilotons of Carbon Dioxide Equivalent (CO2e) into the atmosphere but recapture 154,060 kilotons.[3] Even without carbon accounting rules that attribute emissions from oil extraction to the countries where oil is used, not where it's produced, Guyana is a carbon-negative country and that status is expected to continue.

In a 2024 interview, the BBC's Stephen Sackur challenged the Guyanese President Dr Irfaan Ali about the country's choice to develop its oil and gas resources. Dr Ali in turn asked him: 'Are you aware that Guyana is home to a forest the size of England and Scotland combined?

A forest that stores 19.5 gigatonnes of carbon? A forest that we have preserved?... I am going to lecture you on climate change because we have kept this forest alive that stores 19.5 gigatonnes of carbon that you enjoy, that the world enjoys, that you don't pay us for, that you don't value, that you don't see a value in, that people of Guyana has kept alive.'[4]

The interview excerpt understandably went 'viral' online.[5] It demonstrates the seductiveness of simplistic, easy narratives about a reality that is messy, with geopolitics and climate and emissions intertwined in complicated ways.

Geography is destiny

The resolve of some countries' leaders to realize this destiny is quite evident. The resulting changes once again underline how geopolitics is also not separable from technological change, one of the other major forces changing boardroom conversations in addition to the climate conversation.

China is the world's largest digital economy, with an equally large appetite for energy to power the computing and data infrastructure that underpins that digital economy. Foreign companies operating in China are also required to keep any data on the Chinese consumer in accordance with 2016 Chinese cybersecurity law, inside China.[6]

In 2021 China announced its ambitious Eastern Data, Western Computing (EDWC) plan.[7] Tech companies have so far chosen to locate cloud and data centres near customers in densely populated, major metropolitan regions in the east. China's western regions are less densely populated, with lower land and energy costs, the latter due to abundance of energy resources including coal, natural gas, solar, and wind potential. The goal of the EDWC plan is to enable a nationwide information technology network so that data centres in China's western inland areas process the computing load generated in the eastern coast areas.[8] Major direct investment has come from three state-owned telecom enterprises, with additional investment mobilized from other entities, including private capital.

As part of China's plan to transform 'the roof of the world' – Tibet – into a strategic location for sustainable supercomputing, a computing centre named Yajiang-1 is up and running as of summer 2025.[9] Situated at an altitude of 3,600 meters (11,800 feet), along the river Yarlung Tsangpo, this first major hub of the EDWC plan is designed to be an energy-efficient computing centre, taking advantage of the region's extreme environment, harnessing the natural cold, solar power, and waste heat recovery.

The UAE is another example of geographical destiny meeting strategic thinking. The discovery of oil in 1958 catalysed economic change, making the UAE a big player in the global energy market. The wealth generated also helped develop the UAE's infrastructure with modern roads, ports, and cities. The UAE is now an important financier and strategic partner to many nations, as described elsewhere in this chapter. A substantial amount of funding, reported to be around US$1.5 trillion, has gone into creating G42, a holding company that underpins the Emirates's ambition as an AI and technology superpower. It is chaired by Sheikh Tahnoun bin Zayed al Nahyan, the UAE's national security adviser, underscoring the link between national security, national strategy, and technological advancement.[10]

> Strategic opportunities and possible risks arise from a nation's geography. Where these opportunities intersect with nature, they also collide with climate change, requiring boardrooms to navigate much complexity.

Demographic dividend and the geopolitics of people

A global demographic change – shaped by falling fertility and falling mortality – is currently underway. The world's population is expected to peak at around 10.3 billion people in the mid-2080s, and projected to start declining gradually, falling to 10.2 billion people by the end of the 21st century.[11] More than half of all deaths globally are projected to occur at age 80 or beyond by the late 2050s.[12]

At the same time, the current global fertility rate is at 2.25 live births per woman, down from 3.31 births in 1990. More than half of all countries have fertility below the replacement level of 2.1 live births per woman, and in 45% of countries, the fertility level is at or above 2.1 live births per woman. China, Italy, the Republic of Korea, and Spain are experiencing ultra-low fertility, with fewer than 1.4 live births per woman over a lifetime. The buoyant exceptions – the Central African Republic, Chad, the Democratic Republic of the Congo, Niger, and Somalia – have fertility levels of four births or more per woman. Africa is also the youngest continent in the world, with over 40% of the population in sub-Saharan Africa being below 15 years of age.[13]

The increased life expectancy at birth is expected to contribute to population growth or at least mitigate population decline. In 50 countries, immigration is projected to help arrest the decline in population caused by sustained low levels of fertility and an older age structure. Immigration is also expected to be the main driver of population growth in 52 countries through 2054 and in 62 through 2100, including Australia, Canada, and the USA.

Ageing populations, especially in the west, can – and need to – remain economically productive for a longer time. There is no discernible loss of productivity and in fact in the AI future, the older workforce brings vital human abilities including verbal skills, better reasoning, and visual and spatial intelligence. Also, continued myelin growth and bilateralization of the brain counter the effect of ageing and aid cognitive processing in older persons.[14] Judgement – mainly knowledge combined with the ability to make connections and see the big picture – also improves and older persons are generally happier.[15] This sits right beside the need in many economies worldwide to create meaningful and decently paid jobs for the younger population.

Natalism has not had much success as a policy measure despite many leaders of nations and businesses being increasingly vocal about it. Policy measures supporting natalism extend financial and social incentives for people to have more children. These include tax breaks, baby bonuses, child benefits, and paid parental leave, but in aggregate they do not come close to the cost of raising a child. Some countries have tried to implement more interventionist natalist policies, albeit with limited success. The social structures that support having and bringing up children are expensive and that discourse is difficult to have when so many other demands are being made on the public purse.[16]

> The demographic dynamic, including the need to address declining populations in certain countries which are also ageing, is creating complex societal and business conundrums. Boards must also be cognizant of the forces accelerating migration – wars and climate change – as they will have sizeable impact on businesses' ability to operate and serve meaningfully.

Geopolitics of minerals (and supply chains that underpin energy security and defence)

The long-horizon thinking of the Chinese state is evident in the power and the leverage the country now has in the rare earths sector. China mines 70% of the global rare earths, refines 90% of the rare earth magnets used worldwide, and consumes most of them.[17]

In April 2025, in response to tariffs proposed by the USA, China brought about export restrictions on seven rare earths[18] and related magnet materials.[19] Rare earths and their related magnets are critical components in the electronics, heavy machinery, automotive, and defence sector supply chains. There are also restrictions on other strategic materials such as gallium, germanium, antimony, graphite, and tungsten,[20] crucial to chip manufacturing, which in turn is crucial to the Generative AI boom.

Export licenses are issued for six months and exports are tracked for no-resale and for compliance with restrictions on military use. The scope of the controls is reportedly widening due to the complexity of the supply chain and the inspections, testing, and analysis that can be triggered by the inclusion of rare earths in other products.

The other resource-rich nations, primarily on the African continent, are also changing their approach to allowing access to their natural resources. In 2025, Burkina Faso's leader Captain Ibrahim Traore halted the country's export of minerals to western countries,[21] completing the nationalization of five gold mining assets.[22] Burkina Faso is rich in natural resources, particularly gold and other minerals. Gold produced in Burkina Faso is 2% of the global supply and makes up 18% of the country's GDP, making this policy change a bold move in national sovereignty. An OHADA member state, Burkina Faso ended the presence of French special forces on its land in 2023 and is seeking closer alignment with Russia.

National and business responses to these developments vary from diplomatic moves to investments and innovations.

With an eye on mineral resources, the USA has brokered a peace deal between DR Congo, perhaps the world's richest country in mineral resources including diamonds, gold, coltan (from which niobium and tantalum are extracted), and copper, and Rwanda, with mineral resources such as tantalum, tin ore, tungsten, and gold the second-biggest contributor to its economy after tourism.[23] Closer to home, the Pentagon in the USA has reportedly made a US$400 million direct investment, through preferred stock, taking a 15% stake in MP Materials.[24] The Department of Defence has a warrant to purchase additional shares. MP Materials, based in Las Vegas, is a USA producer extracting rare earths such as neodymium and praseodymium, used in weapons systems and electric vehicles.

The United Arab Emirates and the Central African Republic have signed an economic partnership agreement which will underpin the UAE's investment in defence, agriculture, and mining in the CAR.[25] The UAE has pledged considerable sums of money as investments in logistics, technology, renewable energy, agriculture, and real estate. For instance, the UAE invested US$35 billion in Egypt which helped stabilize the Egyptian economy, averting a currency crisis, and went on to be used to develop Egypt's Mediterranean coastline for tourism.[26] UAE-based companies are also investing in Egypt, Morocco, South Africa, and Kenya, countries in a special free trade agreement with the UAE. These engagements in turn enable the UAE to diversify away from oil into renewable energy.

Saudi Arabia and Oman are the other leading gulf states reshaping the critical minerals landscape.[27] Saudi Arabia has made investments in mining and infrastructure development, and its geological surveys are showing promising reserves of metals needed for everything from electric vehicle batteries to solar panels. The country is also well-positioned to become a logistical hub with its ports offering transit to the USA and Europe.

The challenge for mining critical minerals is in finding both economically and environmentally sustainable ways of operating, an area of developed expertise and experience in Australia and Canada; this would suggest the possibility of new alliances and agreements, challenged as of summer 2025 by the ongoing USA tariff indecisions.

Businesses in the west are investing in advanced separation and recycling technologies including short-loop and long-loop recycling, and electric vehicles (EV) and BESS battery recycling. For instance, Ascend Elements in the USA is working to produce advanced battery materials using valuable elements reclaimed from discarded lithium-ion batteries. Others are collaborating with manufacturers to design products with a focus on recyclability, and yet others are establishing reverse supply chains to encourage consumers to return electrical and electronic products to the manufacturer for recycling.

> Minerals essential to a technology-led climate-resilient future may become cornerstones of future competitiveness. Boards need to consider the associated risks and opportunities.

Geopolitics of alliances and systems that underpin cooperation and trade

Nearly 150 countries joined China's Belt and Road Initiative despite the USA trying to dissuade them. Almost 85% of the world's population did not impose sanctions on Russia despite their condemnation of the Russian invasion of Ukraine; indeed India's share of oil imports from Russia grew from 0.2% to 40%.[28] These are recent examples of the Global South – with its vast diversity encompassing South Americans, Africans, Arabs, and Asians – exercising its agency, signalling a change from passive participation to being active, pragmatic shapers of their own destiny, and a new global order.

Several alliances have emerged – some regional, some broader in geographical scope, some trade agreements, some broader in strategic scope. These include the Association of South East Asian Nations (ASEAN), BRICS (originally Brazil, Russia, India, China, South Africa, countries joined together in an investment thesis), the China–Japan–Korea (CJK) trilateral agreement, the Regional Comprehensive Economic Partnership (RCEP) in Asia-Pacific, the Shanghai Cooperation Organisation (SCO), and the Gulf Cooperation Council (GCC). The Trans Pacific Partnership (TPP) in the Pacific Rim was never ratified but gave way to the Comprehensive and Progressive Agreement for Trans-Pacific Partnership (CPTPP). There is also the definitely-not-Global-South European Union (EU) now seeking multilateral engagement beyond the west, wary of competing with the very same nations in everything from AI to industry, while also seeking access to their buoyant markets. A potentially multipolar world is emerging.

These alliances vary in their strengths with respect to the size of their populations and markets, financial power, technological advancement, energy and climate leadership, and regulation. For instance, the ASEAN has over 700 million people which is the equivalent of the world's fifth largest economy by purchasing power.[29] BRICS is now a powerful alliance of over half of the world's population and almost 40% of the world's economy,[30] with 10 member states and several partner states. It is an alliance sufficiently powerful to draw trade and tariff threats from the President of the United States.

The alliances seek to align their interests to ensure stability, security, and cooperation with a goal to deliver better opportunities, jobs, and quality of life for their citizens. The SCO covers a quarter of the world's area and over 40% of the world's population. It includes a regional anti-terrorist structure to coordinate counter-terrorism and action against separatism and religious extremism, even though the member states do not always agree amongst themselves on designating organizations as 'terrorist groups'. These judgements further do not necessarily align with the western view on matters of extremism and terrorism.

Some such as the CJK focus on the regional economy and disaster relief but also play a key role in global supply chains; the GCC leads on traditional energy sources but increasingly also on providing sovereign funding to develop renewables and technology leadership.

In summer 2025, Brazil and China agreed to explore the feasibility of a transcontinental railway in South America, connecting Brazil's Atlantic Ocean coast to Peru's Pacific Ocean port of Chancay, potentially reducing shipping times to Asia by 12 days.[31]

China also began rebuilding Cuba's national power grid – with funding to support the construction of 55 solar power plants, with plans to add 37 more by 2028, providing two-thirds of Cuba's electricity needs. China has supplied solar panels, steel, tools, and machinery parts for these projects, quietly filling the void left by Cuba's former benefactor Russia being embroiled in a long war with Ukraine.

Africa remains of great strategic interest to both of the world's most populous nations. Indeed China has recently expanded its preferential trade policy, granting zero-tariff access to 53 African countries which is seen as beneficial to Africa.[32]

Both India[33] and China[34] are wooing Ghana, a nation rich in industrial minerals, precious metals (mainly gold), and hydrocarbons. India and Ghana have had formal diplomatic ties since 1957, with a trading relationship where India imports gold and cocoa, and exports electrical goods, machinery, automobiles, and pharmaceuticals. China and Ghana's ties date back to 1960, and Ghana exports cocoa, cashews, and shea butter as well as gold and lithium to China. Both China and India are amongst the top investors in Ghana.

The IMF had advised Namibia to improve its payment systems before rolling out a CBDC; Namibia has now licensed India's UPI technology to enable that. Prime Minister Modi of India is positioning India as a strategic partner to shape 'a future marked by dialogue, equity and cooperation' and says that Africa should not just be seen as 'a source for raw materials'.[35]

With several initiatives – such as trading in local currencies, development of a decentralized digital payment messaging system (BRICS Pay) to rival and bypass SWIFT, institutions such as New Development Bank to finance infrastructure projects – BRICS is increasingly leading in creating a strong alternative to the Bretton Woods System. Countries such as Turkey and Serbia, experiencing frustration with the EU, are also interested in BRICS. Countries in the Global South are increasingly swapping out US$-denominated loans to reduce borrowing costs,[36] pegging to the Renminbi or the Swiss France instead.

Last but not least, the shifting power equations and uncertainties related to tariffs and sanctions mean that in 2025, China, India, and Russia have aligned to provide an alternative – non-western – worldview.[37]

> These moving alliances are geoeconomics in action. Keeping track of the possibilities created by these alliances while also seeking to understand their emergent and dynamic nature are both skills needed in boardrooms worldwide.

Geopolitics of defence and war

It is not controversial to say that since the Second World War, the west, particularly Europe, has enjoyed a life of peace and prosperity, aided in more recent years by a period of low interest rates and globalization. This meant that defence spending remained a relatively small percentage of GDP for most members of NATO. Even on a per-capita basis, the spend was smaller than the defence spend of the USA, a fact that has led to reflection and re-evaluation since the 2022 Russian invasion of Ukraine.[38] A notable development was the shift in investor opinion on defence stocks and their exclusion on ESG-related grounds.[39] As western nations shipped armaments to Ukraine, the debate moved to asking whether investors should take a less exclusionary view of a sector enabling democratic governments in protecting societal values. It is a difficult task to assess, let alone quantify meaningfully, the environmental costs of warfare whether harm is being visited upon natural resources, on man-made infrastructure, or on human beings themselves.

As of 2025, the increased defence spend by NATO member states is a multifaceted strategic decision – to reduce reliance on the USA but also to boost the slow-growing European economies by rebuilding, retooling, and repurposing industry. For instance, in Germany, Rheinmetall plans to convert two German car plants to focus on defence production, and French train maker Alstom has sold its Görlitz plant in Germany which KNDS[40] will start using to produce assemblies for battle tanks, infantry fighting vehicles, and armoured vehicles. The reliance of the defence sector on China, such as for but not limited to critical minerals, however, cannot be solved by retooling.

Warfare is increasingly a technology-led space.[41] There is also the push-pull playing out between manufacturing armaments that are 'good enough' in large numbers and 'better, complex, innovative' in smaller numbers. Enter the drones. The use of drones enables high precision in reconnaissance, surveillance, and strikes, and can minimize risk to human operators of those drones (hence the terms unmanned aerial vehicle

(UAV) or unmanned aircraft system (UAS)); of course this is worth a mention where there are human operators involved at all, since autonomous drones also are in play. Depending on the size – including battery and payload capacity – drones can cover vast areas at a relatively small cost and cause damage to armed vehicles and tanks costing an order of magnitude more in cost.

Drones can also easily threaten warships that cost many times more. This means that a naval strategy as a way to wage war is curtailed or at least compromised, as seen in the case of Russian attempts to control the Black Sea being thwarted by drones. Drones also easily can be an 'air force' in their own right, downing more expensive war planes.

As a side note – drones also have much dual-use potential. Heavy lifting drones which can carry up to 250 kg of weight are useful in logistics, medical transportation, aerial inspections, disaster relief, and agriculture.

With the best technological capability and the fastest capacity-building humanly possible, European defence will need soldiers.[42] That is when defence and security meet demographic and economic reality. Early recruitment efforts are facing shortfalls.

Positioning these jobs as just jobs – hazardous, but jobs – is necessary. But that brings these jobs in competition with other jobs that demand similar skills but may be able to pay more, offer possibly better job security, and not require risking life and limb. Building reserves through part-time work may also help. Then again, a left-field idea is to learn to recruit by reframing skills. In a time when war is conducted remotely, could the young gamers' skills be repurposed to drone operating?

There may be challenges on other fronts too. There is growing disquiet amongst Europeans about the immigrant numbers arriving at their borders. Some have argued that immigration is a demographic necessity – natalism is expensive, and extracting productivity from the older generations may not include conscripting them as soldiers due to sheer physical limitations of ageing – but its unpopularity is fuelling political upheavals.

At the crossover of immigration into Europe and the need for soldiers, European nations will have to face the challenge posed by the immigrants who may have not integrated and who may have not adapted to the values and mores of the society in which they are now living.[43] Will the unintegrated immigrant agree to be conscripted? If that does not turn out to be the case, how might local populations of young men respond? What does that bode for the societal stability businesses need in order to operate?

> Boards need to consider the economics and social dynamics of war as an active component of their resilience thinking.

Geopolitics of data

In 2018, Apple started to build its first China data centre in Guizhou, jointly with Guizhou-Cloud Big Data (GCBD). To comply with Chinese government policy that Chinese users' data be stored within China, Apple had earlier transferred the hosting of its China iCloud user accounts to GCBD.

In early 2025, the UK government demanded that Apple provide it access to encrypted data stored by Apple users worldwide in its cloud service. This demand was made by the Home Office under the Investigatory Powers Act (IPA), which compels firms to provide information to law enforcement agencies. Apple's stance has always been that a master key to or 'backdoor' in its encryption service would enable bad actors. Apple responded to the UK government's demand by withdrawing their advance data protection feature for Apple users in the UK; this affects nine data categories offered by Apple while 14 others remain encrypted.

In 2024, the government of India adopted a new data localization policy – the Digital Personal Data Protection Act (DPDPA). Companies are required to store Indian users' data within India. Sectors such as banking and finance, healthcare and digital retail have more stringent data localization responsibilities following the adoption of this policy.

Other countries also have clear data localization requirements.[44] In Saudi Arabia, the Saudi Data and Artificial Intelligence Authority (SDAIA) requires certain types of data be stored and processed within the country's borders, for enhanced security and control, especially critical infrastructure and sectors such as finance, healthcare, and government services. In Singapore, while the Personal Data Protection Act (PDPA) does not mandate data storage within Singapore's borders, it has provisions for cross-border data transfers which require businesses to conduct risk assessments, obtain user consent, and implement safeguards to protect the data in the country they may transfer the data to.

Data, it is often said, is the new oil. But data really is the storehouse of new state sovereignty, a new boundary condition established within the World Wide Web, which was originally envisaged as a democratizing and borderless force.

Data sovereignty considerations need to be woven into corporate strategy; businesses must know their data assets and their strategic value, and make appropriate infrastructure decisions to balance security, data protection, and compliance.[45]

Whose intellectual property is it anyway?

In its spring/summer 2026 collection shown at Milan Fashion Week in June 2025, Prada included a 'leather footwear' design. Swift backlash made Prada say that it recognizes that the footwear was inspired by traditional Indian footwear.[46] The Kolhapuri, named after Kolhapur in Maharashtra where they are made, dates back to the 12th century, and is hand-made by artisans. It was awarded Geographical Indication status in 2019.

At Bharat Tex 2025, a textile expo in India where over 120 countries participated, the Indian Prime Minister Narendra Modi highlighted the world's turn towards fashion for environment and empowerment.[47]

He shone a light on India's skilled workforce who are maintaining their craft, and called upon the need to retain the authenticity of handloom craftsmanship in the age of technology. He cited India's long textiles tradition, from weaving to colouring. Those with an interest in the supply chain of some of the best-known European luxury brands have known of these brands' reliance on Indian artisans providing everything from intricate embroidery and beadwork, to woven fabrics, leather, and woodwork. Mr Modi's address was an acknowledgement of those specialized skills as well as a clarion call to lay claim to IP that has belonged in cultures with long-established artistry and skill.

Labubu, the collectible plush toy that took over public imagination in 2025, was created in China as part of The Monsters universe. It is a story in China's growing IP economy – which is about creating fresh products but also drawing upon China's cultural assets to create literature, film and television, gaming, and other products. The use of technologies such as cloud rendering is enabling dissemination of cultural phenomena into the virtual mainstream. In turn, a responsive industrial supply chain creates physical products that become iconic.

The landscape is not simple though. The case of Starbucks allegedly trying to thwart Ethiopia's attempts to protect its coffees is illustrative of imbalances of power and financial muscle; Ethiopia's attempts to trademark in the USA met mixed success – Yirgacheffe was allowed in the USA, while Harrar and Sidamo were deemed not eligible for registration. Eventually in 2006 Starbucks agreed to sign trademark licensing agreements acknowledging Ethiopia's ownership of the Harrar, Sidamo, and Yirgacheffe names, regardless of trademark registration grant, and both parties agreed a framework of cooperation for distribution and marketing of these speciality coffee designations.[48]

The Maasai tribe in Kenya and Tanzania have had their likeness, their name, their bravery, strength, and warrior imagery appropriated by a number of companies selling things from cars to luxury goods. No permission was sought nor compensation offered. With lessons learnt from the Ethiopia experience and funding provided by Comic Relief in the UK to do a feasibility study, the Maasai IP Initiative (MIPI), a collective rights-owning entity representing the Maasai community's interests, was set up. Leaders from the Maasai community in Kenya and Tanzania helped organize the unified legal entity. Early wins included a major luxury car brand and a clothing company each returning the Maasai trademark, which will help create licensing revenues in the future.[49] Meg Brindle, who helped organize MIPI, now wants to use the experience to support other groups including the Cherokee, Navajo, and Tuareg peoples.

A few years ago, Anglo-Australian mining company Rio Tinto, that makes two-thirds of its profits from the Pilbara region in Western Australia, blew up 46,000-year-old Juukan Gorge rock shelters for an iron ore mine. A board-led inquiry followed investor and social backlash. The Chair, the CEO, and two of his deputies had to step down as a result.[50]

> These stories illustrate that nations with rich heritage and traditions of craftsmanship are emerging from the shadows to stake their claim in shaping the world's cultural narrative. Boards may want to be thoughtful and watchful about the potential loss of social and legal licence to operate.[51]

Geopolitics and new brands

As Starbucks reviews its business in China, and considers selling a minority stake, the Chinese coffee brand Luckin Coffee has soft-launched in New York. Offering app-based, pick-up-or-delivery-only service, at better prices than Starbucks, Luckin has chosen two locations for launch. One is near Washington Square Park, in the trendy Greenwich village and the neighbourhood of New York University; the second is in NOMAD, a neighbourhood with historical Beaux-Arts and landmark buildings and fashionable hotels, residential developments, restaurants, bars, and shops. Starbucks is returning to its roots as a sit-down-and-chat-over-coffee look-and-feel with a simplified menu; Luckin is leading with tech-first, minimalist decor, and efficiency, almost like a tech-brand, with a flourish that suits New York, the city that is always in a rush.

Araku Coffee from India has been in Paris's Marais neighbourhood since 2017 and has opened new stores serving speciality coffee since. The aristocratic past of Marais has given way to the neighbourhood now being a cultural beating heart, full of old and new world charm, and a diverse community. Araku serves terroir-mapped coffee from the world's largest certified organic plantation in the Eastern Ghats of India, run by tribal farmers in Araku Valley, a bio-diverse region on the borders of Andhra Pradesh and Odisha in India. The company promotes biodiversity and regenerative agriculture and is recognized as a premium luxury social enterprise, befitting the changing narrative of luxury – a space that has belonged to European brands. Araku's story arc begins in 1999 when the Nandi Foundation engaged with the Adivasis, the indigenous tribal communities, in Araku Valley. The Foundation helped revive coffee plantations, set up a farmers' cooperative, and set up a direct selling model in 2015 so the community did not need to rely on intermediaries. The long-time horizon and strategic commitment are yet again in evidence.

Founded in 1996 in India, bootstrapped by the founder group, and now a global enterprise software brand with customers in 150 countries,[52] Zoho is another powerful success story. Its 55-strong product suite is compliant with several global data privacy and security standards as well as local tax laws, supports 71 languages, and hosts data locally with owned data centres in eight countries. Innovation, strategic foresight, financial independence, and customer focus underpin its growth to a US$1 billion business.[53]

African brands are resurgent too. Nando's, originally from South Africa, is a global favourite in casual dining with over 1,000 restaurants in several countries in Asia and Africa, several Gulf States, and the west. Thebe Ikalafeng, the founder of Brand Africa, makes it clear that 'It is not about being anti-international brands; it's about protecting African brands. It's not being anti-western; it's about being pro-African'.[54]

> Countries in the Global South are no longer just consumers and markets for western producers and products, nor just bit players with low-cost or human-scale advantages. They are assertive as strong creators and brand owners in their own right across a range of consumer and business categories. Boards have a whole new canvas of opportunity in the Global South given this rich experience now available.

***

The current geopolitical turmoil has been in motion several years as we saw institutions and norms, on which many democratic institutions leaned, show their frailty. The rules-based order in the west is faltering under pressure. Public trust in governments is falling as citizens in many countries see the corruption, lack of transparency, institutional capture by cronies and plutocrats, and poor public service delivery as just unacceptable. As power struggles emerge over agenda-setting and over territories, it remains a truism that nation state interests are permanent, and alliances are transient. We are indeed witnessing a historic power transition in process.

In addition to the traditional factors of production – land, labour, capital, enterprise – controlled by governments or business owners or investors, new factors of production are at play – namely culture and data. Culture is collectively owned, whereas the ownership of data is being negotiated as governments have a greater say on how businesses collect, store, process, and commercialize their citizens' data.

Geopolitics and geoeconomics show up in business strategy in many ways but most overtly by shaping the business environment, e.g. through domestic policies including industrial, labour, immigration, environment, controls and governance, export and import, capital controls, and foreign investment regulation. Policies such as tariffs, sanctions, and multilateral security agreements shape the trading environment. And then there are the laws that are almost always catching up with emerging technologies including data, IP, and cyber.

Business strategy must evolve in this complex, ever-changing, competitive, and decentralized environment. Keeping up competently with the shifting alliances would lend agility to strategic decision-making as well as operational tactics.

Understanding risk – compound, cascading, emerging, and rapidly changing – is a critical skill, but so are operational agility and strategic readiness that can see and seize the opportunities. Governance frameworks need to be robust to the challenge.

As the clamour to speed up de-dollarization and deglobalization grows, countries are going to try and secure resources. Many countries have begun to stockpile, notably purchasing gold through their central banks.[55,56] Poland, Turkey, India, and China lead the buyer league, while most in Europe including the UK have not changed their stance, and yet others such as Philippines, Kazakhstan, Finland, and Singapore sold some gold. While the buying has been an upward trend since the global financial crisis of 2008, it may be being accelerated as a de-dollarization hedge, security against changes in international settlement systems, economic and monetary uncertainty, and strengthening sovereignty in a geopolitically turbulent environment. Minerals and crude stockpiling are also underway at the time of writing.

Businesses need basic stability and peace in order to continue operating. All these trends are high risk; notably from history, every time there has been deglobalization, there has been war. War-gaming of strategic scenarios sounds like a whole different exercise against this backdrop.

> To navigate the emerging new world order, shifts in power and agendas, and geoeconomic considerations, boards need a future-ready mindset, a broader lens, more fluency, not less, in global cultures and traditions, and a whole new mental model of the world to navigate this emergent uncharted space.

दुःखमित्येव यत्कर्म कायक्लेशभयात्त्यजेत् ।
स कृत्वा राजसं त्यागं नैव त्यागफलं लभेत् ॥ 18-8 ॥
कार्यमित्येव यत्कर्म नियतं क्रियतेऽर्जुन ।
सङ्गं त्यक्त्वा फलं चैव स त्यागः सात्त्विको मतः ॥ 18-9 ॥

To give up prescribed duties because they are troublesome or cause bodily discomfort is renunciation in the mode of passion. Such renunciation is never beneficial or elevating. When actions are undertaken in response to duty, and one relinquishes attachment to any reward, O Arjun, it is considered renunciation in the nature of goodness. (Bhagavad Gita: Chapter 18, Verses 8 and 9)

The following chapter makes the case for a bias for action in service of stewardship, where the fruit of our actions would not accrue to us as board directors, but to the future generations for whom we seek to preserve and accrete financial and other wealth.

7

How it's going...

The current disruptions and discontinuities present us with a smorgasbord of possibilities and provocations for stewardship. These demand, indeed can catalyse, strategic renewal far greater than tinkering on the edges of a five-year strategic plan can. Boards of the future need strategic stamina, not just a compliance mindset.

With change afoot, the board agenda needs to be reset and reinvented – not just what topics show up, but also how they are surfaced to the agenda, how they underpin the conversation on strategy and the future, and how the board's time and attention are apportioned to them.

As innovations speed up alongside BAU, boards need to balance dynamically the needs of today, i.e. incremental value creation opportunities, with the needs for tomorrow and the days beyond that, i.e. continual reinvention with bold steps. In other words, managing allocation of attention and resources along both short and long time horizons to deliver true stewardship.

With increasing complexity, strategic reinvention demands a non-traditional way of thinking. That requires both smarter, bolder board construction as well as building a board culture that appreciates, elicits, and deploys that thinking to stewarding the business's future strategic relevance.

What might all this look like?

Reset the agenda

The political is the strategic

China is strategic about its landmass, with the state as the sponsor and lead investor, bringing clarity of vision and bold implementation; west Asia and the Gulf States deploy their wealth from extractive activities strategically into renewal and renewables. Africa can utilize its demographic advantage to help rebalance the demographic collapse in the west. However, the second- and third-order impacts need to be considered proactively. What impacts of at-scale emigration to the west from the Global South are on your board's radar?

The social unrest – resulting from the lack of cultural integration and cohesion of immigrants, and leading to conflict – brewing in European host countries has been mentioned. What about on the other side, the resurgent Global South?

When skilled professionals emigrate, the Global South loses specialty skills but also witnesses a perverse transfer of wealth, as higher-income countries save money by importing doctors and nurses, many of whom have benefited from subsidized education in their home countries. Empirical data suggest that while businesses and innovation bear short-term negative impacts in the origin countries, over time the emigrants build trade and investment relationships to facilitate knowledge transfer.[1] This opens a new way to collaborate and innovate, and create value.

> A strategic view of the Global South not just as a market, but as an innovation hub and a talent incubator, needs to be on every board's agenda, both in the Global South and elsewhere.

The information environment has changed

Businesses have always navigated changes in the information environment. The web, social platforms, and search engines democratized information dissemination. Echo chambers and filter bubbles leading to social polarization along ideological lines are already very real. A large number of LLM tools at our fingertips has muddied the waters further.

Probabilistically linking words and sentences without considering meaning makes LLMs 'stochastic parrots', argue some AI researchers.[2] While knowledge has never been neutral, LLMs are now deciding on which facts, perspectives, and questions may be surfaced, while suppressing others. Indeed the owner of X, formerly Twitter, posted on 21 June 2025:[3] 'We will use Grok 3.5 (maybe we should call it 4), which has advanced reasoning, to rewrite the entire corpus of human knowledge, adding missing information and deleting errors.' Meanwhile a movement called effective accelerationism rejects the ethics and risks of AI. This is consolidation of epistemic power.

Generative AI companies are forging ahead, training their LLMs on the intellectual property (IP) created by authors, musicians, film makers, and artists, without paying consideration or compensation. The pendulum seems to have swung away from concerns about intellectual monopoly capitalism,[4] where IP protection could lock in monopoly powers from intangible assets even in global value chains.

Legal cases brought by creators against Generative AI companies are mixed and often confusing in their findings.[5] In one case, a federal judge in San Francisco ruled that Anthropic's use of books without permission to train its artificial intelligence system was legal under 'fair use' provisos of USA copyright law, and what it did with them was transformative. Anthropic subsequently agreed to pay authors a US$1.5 billion settlement,[6] which a judge called a 'chaotic mess', while critics feel Anthropic got away cheaply.[7] In the case brought by 13 authors against Meta, the judge ruled in favour of the company, but focused on whether Meta had harmed the market for the author's work. He also made clear that the ruling only affected the rights of the 13 authors who sued, not the many others whose works Meta used to train its models, and did not endorse Meta's use of copyrighted materials as lawful.

Disney and NBC Universal have brought a case against Midjourney which is different from the above two in that their case does not focus on fair use, training data, or text models; instead it focuses on unauthorized generation of original characters. Midjourney allegedly declined to use tools such as prompt filtering and output screening to manage creator rights responsibly.[8] Warner Brothers subsequently brought about a similar lawsuit against Midjourney alleging that Midjourney does little to stop infringement of copyrighted material by its users.[9]

While lawsuits continue, Generative AI companies consolidate not only epistemic power but also wealth creation from controlling the value chain. This breeds a new kind of inequality.

> How is your board taking this dramatically changed information environment into account – for protecting the business's most closely guarded secrets, and for addressing stakeholder engagement on the complex and evolving subject? What does the adoption and integration of LLMs as assistants and collaborators for humans mean for IP creation and ownership? What will the competitiveness of nations and businesses mean in this context? These existential questions need to be on every board's agenda.

The nature of work is changing

The nature of work, value extraction, and the associated risk landscape are all in flux.

With businesses under pressure to grow revenue, profits, and share price all the time, new models emerge. New roles and titles may be created.

A left-field example is the game of cricket. The game's governing body in India organizes the Indian Premier League, which is a highly successful commercial venture. The support teams have evolved tremendously from the time of the traditional five-day test match.[10] They now consist of a head coach or high-performance director, supported by specialist coaches in batting, bowling, and fielding; specialists in sports science and medicine, encompassing strength and conditioning, mobility and movement, physiotherapy, massage therapy, dietetics and nutrition; performance data analysis and innovation; and video and opposition analysts.

Similarly in business, technology systems and infrastructure-related roles are now highly specialized. What was historically an IT function is now split into information technology, operating technology, product technology, and customer technology; they are being led and developed by people with very different skillsets. Equally a CIO, a CTO, a CISO, and increasingly a CDO or Chief AI Officer in the same organization are not uncommon. Whom do these roles report to? What board-level interface or exposure do they have? Via whom – which is worth asking because surely each one of these roles cannot have a seat in the boardroom? How is that 'spokesperson' synthesizing insight from all of these roles and functions?

New contractual models, e.g. gig workers, have emerged too. Their legal status is not settled – companies want to treat them as 'independent contractors', and not 'employees', which would give them rights to benefits such as overtime, sick pay, and insurances, and bargaining rights. The former classification appears to support autonomy but there is control exerted via platforms and tools that use opaque algorithms at times to allocate tasks and pricing.

Workflows themselves have also changed in terms of how a task starts. For instance, an experienced professional planning travel starts with destination and budget, while a younger employee in the same space may look at their favourite TikTok influencer and use their recommendations as a starting point. Many gig workers also leverage tech to their advantage. It is not uncommon to see an Uber driver in India with different phones for different ride-share apps such as Ola Cabs or Savaari or BlaBla cars. They pick the next ride based on distance and fare, and the bit you can't always see as a customer in the backseat of the car is how much money is shaved off that possible fare by the ride-share company.

The narrow specialization in certain roles and the task orientation in certain jobs intersect with the growing discourse around Generative

AI. The usefulness of LLMs is seen as two-fold: better productivity/ efficiency and innovation, which may be assisted, enhanced, or autonomously enabled by AI.

A randomized controlled trial in early 2025,[11] albeit with only 16 experienced software developers, found something interesting. Before the study, the developers had expected the AI tools to save 24% of the time needed for their assigned tasks; after completing the tasks, the developers believed that the AI tools had saved them 20% of time on average; but in reality the AI-aided tasks ended up being completed 19% slower than those completed without AI tools. While the AI tools tended to reduce the average time on active coding, testing, or searching for information, more time was needed in prompting, waiting for AI responses, and then reviewing outputs.

How would your board interpret the 20% expected time saving? Would they hear it as a clarion call to reduce headcount by 20%? Or would they see it as an opportunity to accelerate innovation, as time could be reallocated to more creative work? How would they react to finding that the work was actually done 19% slower?

Where AI tools are enhancing and assisting employees or contractors, how would individual performance be assessed and rewarded? Formula 1 racing comes to mind; the balance of the role of the car, widely believed to be 80%, and the role of the driver, the remaining 20%, in a race is often debated. Researchers at the University of Lethbridge and Simon Fraser University found that in a race, the car's role is more like 20%, the driver's input around 15%, the interaction between the driver and team accounts for 30–40%, with random factors explaining the rest.[12] How would an analogous model work with humans and AI tools?

> How will accountability change with more and more human–AI co-working and co-creating? How do you provide oversight to work in the five-generation workplace? How will the board's role of oversight evolve? How is your board thinking about this?

Your brand, your corporate identity is your ambition engine

The Korean electronics brand LG, with their well-known slogan 'Life's Good', leads with human-centred innovation. The delight embodied in the brand's engagement with its customers, present and future, has carried through to their AI incorporation into the products. For LG, AI is Affectionate Intelligence™. This is on-brand for LG.

In summer 2025, *Wired*, the bellwether and rapporteur of tech and digital culture since its inception, ran a four-week immersive summer school in London.[13] It offered participants a chance to engage with frontier technologies and design thinking, and learn to build solutions to real-world problems. In addition to hands-on training, the programme also offered university credits for students. This offering is utterly on-brand for *Wired.*

The trust embodied by the *Wired* brand in all-things-tech-culture has been built over time. This summer school is a great example of the *Wired* brand connecting with the next generation, aligned with their brand's core purpose.

Your brand similarly embodies your corporate purpose. The brand should be on the future-savvy board's agenda, and the board should be asking questions about the brand's relevance.

Who trusts your brand? Why? In the middle of many social platforms, and AI slop on the web, how does your brand cut through the noise to reach the next generation? Is your brand at risk of 'blanding', or is it strong and vivid? What does your brand sound like, look like? Is your brand consistent?

Your brand and your corporate identity are the ambition engine of your purpose, for the next generation. Is your board talking about it actively and imaginatively?

Space is the new strategic frontier

Whether geopolitics, technology, or climate, space belongs on the future-savvy board's agenda.

A modern business's 'stack' stretches, for better or worse, from the bottom of the oceans to outer space now. Criss-crossing the Atlantic and the Pacific and key trade passages such as the Suez Canal are over 900,000 miles of fibre optic cables that are the backbone of the internet and carry over 95% of all data that moves around, enabling businesses, governments, and consumers alike.[14] Each year, several scores of these cables are cut, mostly accidentally by fishing equipment and anchor. But when the world relies on connectivity and all locations are public, these cables are sitting ducks for sabotage. Recent incidents of internet disruptions affecting a dozen African nations, and of similar disruptions in the Baltic states are cautionary tales.[15,16] From sub-oceanic terrains all the way to outer space, every layer has geopolitical negotiation opportunities.

That discussion brings outer space into the picture. As NASA loses personnel, and Europe loses trust in Starlink, public markets, the British and the French governments, and the Indian multinational Bharti Space have all recently invested in Eutelsat. Companies such as New Orbit in the UK are developing ultra-low Earth orbit satellites that can fly at one-third the altitude of conventional satellites. It would make direct-to-device data possible, and enable better imagery and better weather prediction.

The African Space Agency and the European Commission are parties to a €100 million Space Partnership Programme. The Global Monitoring for Environment and Security (GMES) and Africa programme under its aegis is now part of the African Space Agency; it provides real-time satellite data, empowering many African countries with decision-making tools in climate resilience, disaster response, and marine resource management.[17] Infrastructure investment and unified policy strategies are planned to support Africa's vision for technological sovereignty.

> Regardless of where they operate, businesses reliant on the web need to rethink redundancy and resilience in a whole new way. Has your board reset the resilience discussion?

Business operates in society and society is changing rapidly

Recently in South Africa, a reported 200,000 young people applied for about 5,500 police jobs.[18] In India, youth unemployment stood at over 15% in June 2025.[19] In many western nations, university leavers are struggling to find suitable work. In the EU, the employment rate of 15- to 25-year-olds has fallen over the past two years.[20] AI is cited as one of the reasons – entry-level jobs coming under pressure as work gets automated, from software development to work done by juniors in professional service firms.

Ageism in hiring along with some interesting mental acrobatics and prejudices are revealed by hiring managers in surveys. For instance, the Generation-OECD survey in 2023 found that 47% of hiring managers would hire a candidate age 30–44 for an entry- or intermediate-level role while only 13% said the same about candidates over age 55. Of those same hiring managers, when asked about the job performance of the mid-career and older workers whom they already employ, 89% reported that these individuals performed as well as if not better than younger peers.[21]

Businesses operate in the context of a society where people work and get paid and can then buy their goods and services. The aggregate effect of unemployment in different age groups does not bode well for consumer spend, nor for social stability.

Rapid uptake of technology is challenging assumptions that were once safe. Businesses are, for now, also echoing the message that everything can be generative, and made better and faster with technology.

In the midst of all this, many human beings are trying to work out what it means to live, how to pay for essentials, how to find their vocation, how to find purpose and meaning.

There are serious questions, sometimes wrapped in funny.

> Writer and comedian Matt Somerstein asks:[22] 'can we get some a.i. to pick plastic out of the ocean or do all the robots need to be screenwriters?'

Fantasy and science fiction writer Joanna Maciejewska asks:[23] 'You know what the biggest problem with pushing all-things-AI is? Wrong direction. I want AI to do my laundry and dishes so that I can do art and writing, not for AI to do my art and writing so that I can do my laundry and dishes.'

Businesses need a point of view, one that is aligned with long-term survival of the business but also the long-term survival of the society and the world they are operating in.

The board's agenda needs a reset.

Reimagine the boardroom

The future-savvy boardroom needs those who can help navigate the future-ready agenda, with competence, imagination, and heretical intelligence. These would be thinkers of complexity, and communicators of simplicity, to bring the board and the business along on the journey.

Mindsets and mental models

Uncertainty created by rapid change on many fronts requires a mindset that focuses on the future while calmly navigating the present, and a whole different mental model.

The old mental model underpinning much boardroom decision-making is largely based on an expectation of the future extrapolated from the past, often drawing upon ex-post analytics of past 'big' data. This exercise is often also mixed up with institutional amnesia, outdated data, and loss of tacit knowledge, which happens with executive team changes and board rotations. When the changes underway are of the magnitude and scope we are witnessing, it is worth asking if that mental model holds or whether it needs reframing. The assumptions underpinning current beliefs and approaches need to be questioned for their validity.

The new future demands that boards be more responsive and fleet-footed, using real-time data. Businesses are collecting plenty of data in real time, but who is making sense of it?[24] Through which lenses? Sense-making in uncertainty requires not just being able to deal with vast structured data but also being able to notice small signals that can have an outsized impact either on gathering critical mass or in combination with other, seemingly disparate small signals. Judgement on which small signals deserve attention and which can be safely ignored needs continual attunement.

Fleet-footed does not imply or endorse 'move fast and break things' and disruption and destruction. Fleet-footed is about 'move fast and make things' by creation through collaboration across cultural silos and stereotypes.

> Boardrooms leading future-relevant global strategies will need people who are not cognitively and culturally all alike, and then to meet them on equal and respectful terms. This needs a new set of skills and temperaments around the boardroom table too.

The right temperaments, personalities, and cognitive styles

Who is around the board table? The deep thinker? The idea generator? The provocateur? The contrarian? The consensus builder? The synthesizer? The narrow specialist? The systems thinker?

How many on the board think in straight lines? How many look like they make non-linear leaps? Can they explain those leaps?

How many on the board think inside narrow silos of compliance and functions? How many inhabit the edges and think differently? Deeply embedded sector people frame and imagine things very differently from those living on the edges. It is worth asking – what problem is the business solving today? What problem might the business solve in the near-future or further-future? How to balance the need to play defence with the need to leapfrog some developments?

Who are your wartime colleagues with the experience and temperament to deal with crises? Who are the ones most effective in peacetime? How does your board put them to use most effectively?

> Technology is reshaping old definitions and boundaries, while geopolitical changes are demanding a whole new *Weltanschauung*. The boardroom needs a different set of fluencies and ways of working for this emergent future.

Geo-sensibilities

Boards need a range of geo-sensibilities – *geopolitics*, which is an understanding of geographical location, terrain and topology, spatial relations, and how all these shape power rivalry between nation states and the security landscape; *geostrategy*, which is about how states navigate geopolitical constraints and opportunities to advance their national interests; and *geoeconomics*,[25] which is about understanding how governments use their countries' economic strength from existing financial and trade relationships, and tools such as sanctions, trade, finance, risk, and war, to achieve geopolitical and economic goals.

Business strategy is bound up in these considerations – for monitoring and managing risks, but also for taking advantage of opportunities. Decisions about location, corporate form, data strategy, and governance are inseparable from a nation state's political stability, business climate, consumer demand, growth opportunities, and quality of talent.

Geopolitical disruptions have shaped some well-known examples of relocation. The non-profit RISC-V Foundation relocated to Switzerland over concerns about restrictions on their core technology in the USA–China trade war;[26] British electrical manufacturer Dyson moved its headquarters to Singapore following Brexit, citing British suppliers not wanting to grow with Dyson;[27] British car maker Lotus is also said to be exploring strategic options following the tariffs uncertainty in the USA in 2025;[28] and Proton, the Swiss provider of encrypted email and VPN services, began relocating its physical strategic assets to Germany and Norway in the face of a Swiss draft bill that may compel mandatory user identification and data retention.[29]

> Smart boardrooms take cognizance of cultural and social contracts, often not explicitly codified, just tacit and implicit; the translators mentioned elsewhere in this section can help make the tacit more understandable. Are they at your boardroom table?

Strategic imagination, not just strategic planning

Strategy requires imagination to see possibilities. Foresight too requires imagination. As does the need to protect brand and board reputation.

As sources of risk grow and evolve, particularly to data in motion or at rest on our servers or cloud instances, how does the board monitor compound risks? For instance, cyber risk is made worse by the deployment of AI in broadening how cyber attacks are perpetuated. Aside of the risks of malicious prompt injection and LLM jailbreaking, securing AI agents is fundamentally harder than securing traditional systems, because they don't operate on static logic. They learn, evolve, and act based on dynamic inputs.

Meanwhile, cyber criminals are becoming more sophisticated in their business and operating models. State sponsors of cyber crime also take advantage of the fact that no major nation state wants to call a state-backed cyber attack 'an act of war' and do anything visible to counter such attacks.

Can someone on the board think like a Bond villain, who has an outcome focus, can commandeer the right resources, has an understanding of the negative externalities, but also keeps an eye on long-term strategic objectives?

A stomach for uncertainty

How does the board make decisions when things are emerging and changing rapidly, with unpredictable costs or the need to experiment with staged funding? As an example, decisions to support Generative AI implementation come with several spend decisions on hardware, data, and talent, with both expected returns and the time horizon to returns being uncertain.

Boldness, not recklessness. As mentioned elsewhere, regulations and governance can provide guardrails but they should not serve solely to throttle and derail the need to build better.

Understanding and unpacking complexity

As board directors, we are overseeing complexity – physical, social, and increasingly biological. Components of a complex system interact with one another and with their environment. In other words there are dependencies, competitions, and other relationships between the components, the system, and the environment in various combinations.

These systems also self-organize; some adapt, some may show critical transitions, e.g. the financial system contagion seen during the financial crises in our time. Criticality does not always arrive rapidly but may develop over time, arising from the connectedness of the component parts. Horizon-scanning plays a key role in ensuring it does not come as a surprise when it does crystallize.

Sometimes, different complex systems interact in imaginative ways that can reshape your business or even your industry. The availability and widespread uptake of GLP1 drugs for diabetes and then for weight loss has had an impact on the food industry, with people consuming more fruits and vegetables and drastically fewer sugary and alcoholic drinks.[30] These effects have required supermarkets to adapt their inventory to new consumer preferences. Other industries such as healthcare providers may see impact down the line.

> The boardroom of the future requires the skills essential to understanding and explaining complexity: systems thinking, an understanding of positive and negative feedback loops, and imagination.

Polyglots in the boardroom

A recent collaboration between Africa No Filter and Dr Adam Hahn of the University of Bath found that the day-to-day perception of Africa in the UK and the USA is still largely shaped by outdated and negative stereotypes; this reductive framing of course has profound consequences for how people engage with the continent culturally and economically.[31] Africa is not just a large market for western products, but a continent with a rich cultural tapestry and a vibrant young population, building brands and businesses in many categories.

The African Union is supporting a campaign by Africa No Filter and Speak Up Africa, for wider adoption of a world map using Equal Earth projection instead of the Mercator projection.[32] The latter inflates the size of regions away from the equator and can lead to an underestimation of the African continent's potential, distorting investment decisions, while the former, albeit imperfect in representing a spherical world on a flat map, may represent Africa more accurately.

How to navigate this need to change perspective?

Boards could invite polyglots, those who speak and understand several languages. Languages provide access to different worlds, so to speak, and help break stereotypes. These polyglots may be literal, such as the BBC's Steve Rosenberg, Lyse Doucet, and Katya Adler. These three journalists respectively report on Russia, Ukraine, and Belarus; Afghanistan and west Asia; and Europe. They speak the languages – albeit as non-native speakers – that enable their access and that access makes their reportage possible and meaningful. Polyglots could be the new cultural translators that boardrooms need, to understand the emerging world order a little bit better.

Not all polyglots however are literally multilingual rapporteurs or journalists. Those who cross cultural and disciplinary silos are polyglots too. They know how to translate between different disciplines' lingos and make ideas more accessible. Breakthrough innovation often lies at the cusp of disciplines, catalysed by people with a range of skills and perspectives coming together, navigating the diffuse space with unclear priors, as many of the stories in the book show.

> Boards seeking technical skills and sector knowledge may need to expand their dialogue with prospective directors. Temperament and character need to be probed more, though not reduced to psychometric testing. It is worthwhile understanding the fires that forged their temperament and character. What sorts of uncertainties have they navigated? How do they seek and then process information? How do they regulate themselves in duress, uncertainty and chaos? What has all that experience taught them about themselves? And finally, how can they use that experience to help the boardroom navigate the changing context in which the business is operating?

Ticking away the moments…

The question of the time horizon is a critical element in the stewardship discourse.

Board directors' time on the board may be term-limited, or not – a time horizon of professional and personal self-interest. But the entire job of boards is to create long-term success and the impact of their work has longer time horizons – longer than a business or economic cycle. The rapid changes brought by technological advancement upend all time horizons, speeding most of them up. The geopolitical changes we are witnessing are making time seem elastic and fluctuating from day to day.

One thing is undeniable: time is a non-renewable resource, served in 24-hour daily dollops.

Here on, it all gets philosophical quickly.

The whole job of stewardship is that we aim for progress and betterment, not just for personal kudos or credit, and that we accept we will not necessarily be here to enjoy or witness the outcome. We make a minuscule contribution in the grand scheme of things. We are both a twinkle in our mothers' eyes and a speck of dust somewhere admixed with nature. In between those two moments are our decisions and our stewardship.

Let's make them count.

Notes

Preface

[1] I use 'Chair' to signify the person chairing the board, throughout this book. Some Chairs including women Chairs whom I have interviewed for the book like to be referred to as Chairman, and do not see the term as gendered.

1 How it started...

[1] With apologies to Bruce Lee whose last film was titled *Enter the Dragon* and with thanks to Nurole, the UK's leading board headhunting firm, whose famous podcast 'Enter the Boardroom™' featured me as a guest in October 2023.
[2] The report can be found here: https://policyexchange.org.uk/publication/bittersweet-success-glass-ceilings-for-britains-ethnic-minorities-at-the-top-of-business-and-the-professions/ (Accessed: 13 November 2025).
[3] A two-hour duration BESS can provide energy at its maximum power capacity for two hours before needing to be recharged.
[4] In the Indian epic Mahabharata, the character Yudhishthira had the reputation that he never told lies. The war of Mahabharata could turn on his willingness to collaborate on getting the lead warrior, the archery teacher Dronācharya, to lay down his weapons. Desiring victory but not keen to lie, Yudhishthira said on the battlefield that Aswatthāma had been killed, adding the word 'elephant' indistinctly after the name. Hearing this, Dronācharya believed his son, also named Aswatthāma, was killed, and laid down his weapons. This story of obfuscation perhaps comes closest to what the director conveyed by way of his experience.
[5] From French *pantoufle*, meaning slippers.

2 The first 100 days

[1] *Aktiengesellschaft* – company limited by share ownership; shares may be traded on a stock market.
[2] *Gesellschaft mit beschränkter Haftun* – limited liability company.
[3] Shadow director – UK company law defines this as 'a person in accordance with whose directions or instructions the directors of a company are accustomed to act'; they are not listed or formally appointed as a director but exert real

influence over the affairs of the company. Those who advise in a professional capacity such as accountants or lawyers are not considered shadow directors even though they may have influence over the affairs of the company.

[4] *Connective Tissue* (2022) by Shefaly M. Yogendra. Available at: https://shefaly-yogendra.com/2022/04/19/connective-tissue/ (Accessed: 12 September 2025).

3 Inside the boardroom

[1] *Feriae conceptivae*: originally Roman religious holidays which were moveable feasts in that the dates moved but the festivals did get celebrated around the same time every year; colloquially, things that can happen whenever it suits people. Over time, Roman holidays came to signify debauchery and bloodsport.

[2] Fiduciary Duties of Investment Intermediaries. Available at: https://web.archive.org/web/20140924041547/http://lawcommission.justice.gov.uk/areas/fiduciary_duties.htm (Accessed: 7 June 2025).

[3] OHADA – *Organisation pour l'harmonisation en Afrique du droit des affaires* or Organization for the Harmonization of Business Law in Africa.

[4] 'OHADA's existence is credited to the need to attract foreign investment through a legal order that is appealing to the eyes of Western investors' – Minzoto, B. (2024) 'Corporate purpose and governance in Africa: French-influenced OHADA law, local norms, and heterodox pluralism', *Journal of Corporate Law Studies*, 24(2), 437–78. https://doi.org/10.1080/14735970.2025.2449712

[5] Arewa O.B. (2021) *Disrupting Africa: Technology, law, and development.* Cambridge: Cambridge University Press; Rosenthal, C. (2019) *Accounting for Slavery: Masters and Management.* London: Harvard University Press.

[6] *Corporate Governance by Country* (2023), ECGI. Available at: www.ecgi.global/publications/codes/corporate-governance-by-country (Accessed: 12 September 2025).

[7] Palma, S. and Fontanella-Khan, J. (2022) 'US antitrust warnings lead to corporate board resignations', *Financial Times*, 19 October. Available at: www.ft.com/content/879ac962-0a30-488e-a964-a83a9162ead4 (Accessed: 14 September 2025).

[8] *Harvard Business Review* (2025) 'How pioneering boards are using AI', 1 July. Available at: https://hbr.org/2025/07/how-pioneering-boards-are-using-ai (Accessed: 12 September 2025).

[9] Harris, L. and Heikkilä, M. (2025) 'Insurers launch cover for losses caused by AI chatbot errors', *Financial Times*, 11 May. Available at: www.ft.com/content/1d35759f-f2a9-46c4-904b-4a78ccc027df (Accessed: 12 September 2025). Some insurers have recently launched insurance coverage against losses

caused to companies by AI tools hallucinating or making mistakes. As of mid-2025 there is no equivalent D&O insurance product on offer for an AI model as a board director.

[10] Delauney, G. (2025) 'World's first AI minister will eliminate corruption, says Albania's PM', *BBC*, 12 September. Available at: www.bbc.co.uk/news/articles/cm2znzgwj3xo (Accessed: 12 September 2025).

[11] *Welcome to TinyTroupe* (no date) *Github.io*. Available at: https://microsoft.github.io/TinyTroupe/ (Accessed: 12 September 2025).

[12] Relevant readings: Son, Y., Wowak, K.D. and Post, C. (2025) 'From the boardroom to the jobsite: Female board representation and workplace safety', *Journal of Operations Management*, 71(6), 741–62. Available at: https://doi.org/10.1002/joom.1370

(No date) *Fastcompany.com*. Available at: www.fastcompany.com/91353555/more-women-in-the-boardroom-can-lead-to-safer-companies (Accessed: 12 September 2025).

[13] Sier, J. (2023) 'Nuix director concedes he didn't read board papers', *Australian Financial Review*. Available at: www.afr.com/technology/nuix-director-concedes-he-didn-t-read-board-papers-20231208-p5eq1w (Accessed: 12 September 2025).

[14] ASIC is the government agency that oversees the Australian business, finance, and consumer credit sectors. Since 2008 ASIC has used Nuix's e-discovery software as part of its investigative capabilities and is seeking alternatives ahead of its 2027 contract expiry. Dickinson, E. (no date) 'ASIC scopes data forensics future ahead of Nuix deal expiry', *iTnews*. Available at: www.itnews.com.au/news/asic-scopes-data-forensics-future-ahead-of-nuix-deal-expiry-615848 (Accessed: 12 September 2025).

[15] 'ASIC sues Nuix and its board for continuous disclosure and directors' duties breaches' (no date) *Gov.au*. Available at: www.asic.gov.au/about-asic/news-centre/find-a-media-release/2022-releases/22-262mr-asic-sues-nuix-and-its-board-for-continuous-disclosure-and-directors-duties-breaches/ (Accessed: 12 September 2025).

[16] Chande, S. (2020) 'Temple Bar serves protective notice to manager Ninety One UK', *QuotedData*. Available at: https://quoteddata.com/2020/04/temple-bar/ (Accessed: 12 September 2025).

[17] Tew, I. (no date) 'Temple Bar swaps Ninety One for RWC following review', *Ftadviser.com*. Available at: www.ftadviser.com/investments/2020/09/23/temple-bar-swaps-ninety-one-for-rwc-following-review/ (Accessed: 12 September 2025).

[18] Belanger, A. (2025) 'To avoid admitting ignorance, Meta AI says man's number is a company helpline', *Ars Technica*. Available at: https://arstechnica.com/tech-policy/2025/06/to-avoid-admitting-ignorance-meta-ai-says-mans-number-is-a-company-helpline/ (Accessed: 12 September 2025).

[19] (No date). Available at: www.youtube.com/watch?v=I75Ud2W9PkA (Accessed: 17 October 2025).

[20] *Appointment, Election and Removal of Directors* (no date) *Hkexgroup.com*. Available at: www.hkexgroup.com/Corporate-Governance/Corporate-Governance-Framework/Corporate-Governance-Practices/Board-of-Directors/Appointment-and-Election-and-Removal-of-Directors?sc_lang=en (Accessed: 14 September 2025).

[21] Kapoor, S. and Jain, S. (2024) 'Deciphering the Indian boardroom: Russell Reynolds associates' 2024 India board analytics & insights', *Russellreynolds.com*. Available at: www.russellreynolds.com/en/insights/reports-surveys/deciphering-the-indian-boardroom-2024-board-analytics-insights (Accessed: 12 September 2025).

[22] Viviers, S. and Mans-Kemp, N. (2019) 'Director overboardedness in South Africa: evaluating the experience and busyness hypotheses', *International Journal of Disclosure and Governance*, 16(1), 68–81. Available at: https://doi.org/10.1057/s41310-019-00057-x.

[23] (No date) *Harvard.edu*. Available at: https://corpgov.law.harvard.edu/2021/11/13/roundup-of-director-overboarding-policies/ (Accessed: 12 September 2025).

[24] Eagly, A.H. (2016) 'When passionate advocates meet research on diversity, does the honest broker stand a chance?: Passionate advocates and diversity research', *The Journal of Social Issues*, 72(1), 199–222. Available at: https://doi.org/10.1111/josi.12163.

[25] Leung, K. and Wang, J. (2015) 'Social processes and team creativity in multicultural teams: A socio-technical framework', *Journal of Organizational Behavior*, 36(7), 1008–25. Available at: https://doi.org/10.1002/job.2021.

[26] Leung, K. and Wang, J. (2015) 'Social processes and team creativity in multicultural teams: A socio-technical framework', *Journal of Organizational Behavior*, 36(7), 1008–25. Available at: https://doi.org/10.1002/job.2021.

[27] 'The power of diverse thinking: How the best teams make decisions', *Diversityproject.com*. Available at: https://diversityproject.com/wp-content/uploads/2025/06/DP-Cognitive-Diversity-Full-Research-Paper.pdf (Accessed: 12 September 2025).

[28] Sternberg, R.J. (1985) *Beyond IQ: A Triarchic Theory of Human Intelligence*. Cambridge: Cambridge University Press.

[29] (No date) *Harvard.edu*. Available at: https://corpgov.law.harvard.edu/2025/06/23/board-effectiveness-a-survey-of-the-c-suite-4/ (Accessed: 12 September 2025).

[30] (No date) *Economist.com*. Available at: www.economist.com/business/2024/12/12/tesla-intel-and-the-fecklessness-of-corporate-boards (Accessed: 12 September 2025).

[31] 'The opaque ceiling: only half of British employees know what their company board does' (2024) *Lawdebenture.com*. Available at: www.lawdebenture.com/news-insights/the-opaque-ceiling-only-half-of-british-employees-know-what-their-company-board-does (Accessed: 12 September 2025).

[32] Page 4 of (No date) *Org.sg*. Available at: www.sid.org.sg/common/Uploaded%20files/Resources/GNDI_board_performance_evaluation_guideline_2024.pdf (Accessed: 12 September 2025).

[33] Heraclitus, *Allegoriae* 24.5 (Ποταμοῖς τοῖς αὐτοῖς ἐμβαίνομέν τε καὶ οὐκ ἐμβαίνομεν, εἶμέν τε καὶ οὐκ εἶμεν… .) – rough translation: We both step and do not step, we both are and are not, in the same rivers.

[34] (No date) *Harvard.edu*. Available at: https://corpgov.law.harvard.edu/2023/04/27/does-board-size-matter/ (Accessed: 13 September 2025).

[35] King Report on Governance for South Africa 2009. Available at: https://cdn.ymaws.com/www.iodsa.co.za/resource/collection/94445006-4F18-4335-B7FB-7F5A8B23FB3F/King_III_Report.pdf (Accessed: 13 November 2025).

[36] Gardner, H. and Peterson, R. (2019) 'Back channels in the boardroom', *Harvard Business Review* [Preprint]. Available at: https://hbr.org/2019/09/back-channels-in-the-boardroom (Accessed: 12 September 2025).

[37] 'The C-suite's role in well-being' (2022) *Deloitte Insights*. Deloitte. Available at: www.deloitte.com/us/en/insights/topics/leadership/employee-wellness-in-the-corporate-workplace.html (Accessed: 12 September 2025).

[38] Raval, A. (2025) 'Why the serial CEO has fallen out of fashion', *Financial Times*, 23 June. Available at: www.ft.com/content/7bb87f99-882e-477d-90a7-31b16a9aef07 (Accessed: 13 September 2025).

[39] 'What happens if a director becomes mentally incapable?' (no date) *Com.au*. Available at: www.townsendslaw.com.au/blb-news/280/what-happens-if-a-director-becomes-mentally-incapable/ (Accessed: 13 September 2025).

[40] Freer, G. (2018) 'Mental health: Legal pitfalls when dismissing workers with conditions', *Personnel Today*, 16 April. Available at: www.personneltoday.com/hr/mental-health-legal-pitfalls-dismissing-workers/ (Accessed: 12 September 2025).

[41] *Financial Times* (2025) 'In cyber attacks, humans can be the weakest link', 26 May. Available at: www.ft.com/content/4349b16a-8ec1-44d9-a295-3a51523805a8 (Accessed: 12 September 2025).

[42] Smith, S. (2025) 'Marks & Spencer CEO responds to cyber incident', *TheIndustry.beauty*. Available at: https://theindustry.beauty/marks-spencer-ceo-responds-to-cyber-incident/ (Accessed: 13 September 2025).

[43] 'M&S' cyber attack response is brilliant crisis comms' (2025) *Prmoment.com*. #creator. Available at: www.prmoment.com/opinion/m-s-cyber-attack-response-is-brilliant-crisis-comms (Accessed: 13 September 2025).

[44] (No date) *Cybernews.com*. Available at: https://cybernews.com/cybercrime/marks-spencer-breach-class-action-lawsuit/ (Accessed: 13 September 2025).

[45] Extracted from the email to customers sent by M&S on 15 May 2025; also posted on *Cyber Update* (no date) *Marks & Spencer*. Available at: https://corporate.marksandspencer.com/cyber-update (Accessed: 13 September 2025).

[46] Plimmer, G. and O'Dwyer, M. (2021) 'NHS digital under scrutiny for ties with Accenture', *Financial Times*, 9 May. Available at: www.ft.com/content/039f62e0-33e7-4385-81eb-027c0c4ba171 (Accessed: 12 September 2025).

[47] FRC May 2025 register of interests. Available at: https://media.frc.org.uk/documents/Register_of_Interests_May_2025.pdf (Accessed: 12 September 2025).

[48] 'UK directors' duty to avoid conflicts of interest' (2008) *Pinsent Masons*. Available at: www.pinsentmasons.com/out-law/guides/uk-directors-duty-to-avoid-conflicts-of-interest (Accessed: 12 September 2025).

[49] A cap table is a record of a company's ownership structure. This details who owns what percentage of the company and the types of equity they hold. It is essential for understanding ownership dilution, and planning for future fundraising rounds.

[50] Eirola, A., Bezemer, P.-J. and Reinhold, S. (2025) 'Boardroom dissent: An integrative review and future research agenda', *Corporate Governance: An International Review*, 33(3), 389–406. Available at: https://doi.org/10.1111/corg.12607.

[51] Edmans, A. (2025) 'LBS guest speaker on culture and corporate success', *Linkedin.com*. Available at: www.linkedin.com/posts/aedmans_delighted-to-welcome-robert-swannell-cbe-activity-7331581387067510784-6cgJ (Accessed: 12 September 2025).

[52] (No date) *Iea.org*. Available at: www.iea.org/reports/russian-supplies-to-global-energy-markets/gas-market-and-russian-supply-2 (Accessed: 12 September 2025).

[53] (No date) *Parliament.uk*. Available at: https://committees.parliament.uk/oralevidence/10936/html/ (Accessed: 12 September 2025).

[54] Conversion shares or C shares are issued by investment trusts to raise money through new shares without affecting existing shareholders negatively.

[55] (No date) *Brighterir.com*. Available at: https://polaris.brighterir.com/public/harmony_energy_investment_trust/news/rns/story/w137m6r (Accessed: 12 September 2025).
[56] BBC News (2022) 'Cottingham: Europe's biggest battery storage system switched on', *BBC*, 21 November. Available at: www.bbc.co.uk/news/uk-england-humber-63707463 (Accessed: 12 September 2025).
[57] (No date) *Investegate.co.uk*. Available at: www.investegate.co.uk/stock-exch-notice/rns/admission-to-trading---31-01-2023/202301310800013064O/ (Accessed: 12 September 2025).
[58] Plummer, J. (2023) 'Hot Seat: Leading a £274m Knaresborough green energy firm', *The Stray Ferret*. Available at: https://thestrayferret.co.uk/hot-seat-leading-a-274m-knaresborough-green-energy-firm/ (Accessed: 12 September 2025).
[59] T-1 is a one year ahead capacity auction. T-4 is four years ahead capacity auction.
[60] *Morningstar UK: Market News & Investing Advice* (no date) *Morningstar, Inc.* Available at: www.morningstar.co.uk/uk/news/AN_1676915974352011900/harmony-energy-income-trust-extends-credit-terms-as-projects-advance.aspx (Accessed: 12 September 2025).
[61] (No date) *Gov.uk*. Available at: https://assets.publishing.service.gov.uk/government/uploads/system/uploads/attachment_data/file/1140189/review_of_electricity_market_arrangements_summary_of_responses.pdf (Accessed: 12 September 2025).
[62] *Morningstar UK: Market News & Investing Advice* (no date) *Morningstar, Inc.* Available at: www.morningstar.co.uk/uk/news/AN_1682324320583718400/thomaslloyd-requests-share-suspension-due-to-fair-value-uncertainty.aspx (Accessed: 12 September 2025).
[63] *Morningstar UK: Market News & Investing Advice* (no date) *Morningstar, Inc.* Available at: www.morningstar.co.uk/uk/news/AN_1685621190220198000/in-brief-harmony-energy-income-trust-energises-farnham-project.aspx (Accessed: 12 September 2025).
[64] (No date) *Brighterir.com*. Available at: https://polaris.brighterir.com/public/harmony_energy_investment_trust/news/rns/story/x44p4ox (Accessed: 12 September 2025).
[65] (No date) *Brighterir.com*. Available at: https://polaris.brighterir.com/public/harmony_energy_investment_trust/news/rns/story/x2ekplx (Accessed: 12 September 2025).
[66] Gillespie, T. and Nair, D. (2023) 'British energy storage firm Zenobe to grow in US, Australia with $1 billion funding', *Bloomberg News*, 7 September.

Available at: www.bloomberg.com/news/articles/2023-09-07/uk-energy-storage-firm-zenobe-to-grow-in-us-australia-with-1-billion-funding (Accessed: 12 September 2025).

[67] Prime Minister's Office (2023) 'PM speech on Net Zero: 20 September 2023', *Gov.uk*. Available at: www.gov.uk/government/speeches/pm-speech-on-net-zero-20-september-2023 (Accessed: 13 September 2025).

[68] (No date) *Brighterir.com*. Available at: https://polaris.brighterir.com/public/harmony_energy_investment_trust/news/rns/story/ryj0vkr (Accessed: 12 September 2025).

[69] (No date) *Brighterir.com*. Available at: https://polaris.brighterir.com/public/harmony_energy_investment_trust/news/rns/story/w0j3pnx (Accessed: 12 September 2025).

[70] (No date) *Brighterir.com*. Available at: https://polaris.brighterir.com/public/harmony_energy_investment_trust/news/rns/story/wvd59zw (Accessed: 12 September 2025).

[71] (No date) *Brighterir.com*. Available at: https://polaris.brighterir.com/public/harmony_energy_investment_trust/news/rns/story/xl4dd9r (Accessed: 12 September 2025).

[72] (No date) *Brighterir.com*. Available at: https://polaris.brighterir.com/public/harmony_energy_investment_trust/news/rns/story/xz4y93w (Accessed: 12 September 2025).

[73] (No date) *Brighterir.com*. Available at: https://polaris.brighterir.com/public/harmony_energy_investment_trust/news/rns/story/wve00qx (Accessed: 12 September 2025).

[74] (No date) *Brighterir.com*. Available at: https://polaris.brighterir.com/public/harmony_energy_investment_trust/news/rns/story/rgvdz0r (Accessed: 12 September 2025).

[75] (No date) *Brighterir.com*. Available at: https://polaris.brighterir.com/public/harmony_energy_investment_trust/news/rns/story/wk656dx (Accessed: 12 September 2025).

[76] (No date) *Brighterir.com*. Available at: https://polaris.brighterir.com/public/harmony_energy_investment_trust/news/rns/story/x42mypr (Accessed: 12 September 2025).

[77] The Takeover Code requires that 'under Rule 8.3(a) of the Code, any person who is interested in 1% or more of any class of relevant securities of an offeree company or of any securities exchange offeror (being any offeror other than an offeror in respect of which it has been announced that its offer is, or is likely to be, solely in cash) must make an Opening Position Disclosure following the

commencement of the offer period and, if later, following the announcement in which any securities exchange offeror is first identified'.

[78] The Takeover Panel is an independent body in the UK; its main functions are to issue and administer the Takeover Code and to supervise and regulate takeovers and other matters under the Code. Its principal purposes are to ensure fair treatment for all shareholders and an orderly framework for takeover bids.

[79] (No date) *Brighterir.com*. Available at: https://polaris.brighterir.com/public/harmony_energy_investment_trust/news/rns/story/w6om9qw (Accessed: 12 September 2025).

[80] *London Stock Exchange* (no date) *Londonstockexchange.com*. Available at: www.londonstockexchange.com/news-article/HEIT/scheme-of-arrangement-becomes-effective/17088909 (Accessed: 12 September 2025).

[81] (No date) *Brighterir.com*. Available at: https://polaris.brighterir.com/public/harmony_energy_investment_trust/news/rns/story/xlo9n9x (Accessed: 12 September 2025).

[82] Stifel (2024) 'How to interpret the role of a Non-Executive Board', 29 May.

4 You and the algorithm

[1] Apple (2017) *iPhone 8 and iPhone 8 Plus: A New Generation of iPhone*, *Apple*. Available at: www.apple.com/newsroom/2017/09/iphone-8-and-iphone-8-plus-a-new-generation-of-iphone/ (Accessed: 12 September 2025).

[2] Stark, C. (2018) 'Here's a helpful timeline of System on a Chip (SoC) designs by Apple', *Stark Insider*. Available at: www.starkinsider.com/2018/01/heres-timeline-system-chip-soc-models-apple.html (Accessed: 12 September 2025).

[3] Stark, C. (2018) 'Here's a helpful timeline of System on a Chip (SoC) designs by Apple', *Stark Insider*. Available at: www.starkinsider.com/2018/01/heres-timeline-system-chip-soc-models-apple.html (Accessed: 12 September 2025).

[4] Apple (2024) *WWDC24 highlights*, *Apple*. Available at: www.apple.com/newsroom/2024/06/wwdc24-highlights/ (Accessed: 12 September 2025).

[5] Weber, J. (1990) 'Apple to join acorn, VLSI in chip-making venture', *The Los Angeles Times*, 28 November. Available at: www.latimes.com/archives/la-xpm-1990-11-28-fi-4993-story.html (Accessed: 12 September 2025).

[6] *All Waste Types* (no date) *ZenRobotics*. Available at: www.terex.com/zenrobotics/waste-types/overview (Accessed: 12 September 2025).

[7] (No date) *Courthousenews.com*. Available at: www.courthousenews.com/sanctions-ordered-for-lawyers-who-relied-on-chatgpt-artificial-intelligence-to-prepare-court-brief/ (Accessed: 12 September 2025).

[8] (No date) *Lawgazette.co.uk*. Available at: www.lawgazette.co.uk/news/lawyers-escape-contempt-proceedings-over-fake-case-citations/5123511.article (Accessed: 12 September 2025).

[9] 'Margaret Wanjiku' (no date) *Org.uk*. Available at: https://africaprize.raeng.org.uk/2025-cohort/margaret-wanjiku (Accessed: 12 September 2025).

[10] (No date) *Yourstory.com*. Available at: https://yourstory.com/herstory/2020/07/woman-entrepreneur-onion-price-agritech-farmer (Accessed: 12 September 2025).

[11] gov/cto, N. (no date) *The New York City Internet of Things Strategy*, *Nyc.gov*. Available at: www.nyc.gov/assets/cto/downloads/iot-strategy/nyc_iot_strategy.pdf (Accessed: 12 September 2025).

[12] Belanger, A. and Technica, A. (2024) 'Air Canada has to honor a refund policy its chatbot made up', *Wired*, 17 February. Available at: www.wired.com/story/air-canada-chatbot-refund-policy/ (Accessed: 12 September 2025).

[13] Trangle, S. (2025) 'AI may determine the price of your next delta ticket', *Investopedia*. Available at: www.investopedia.com/ai-may-determine-the-price-of-your-next-delta-ticket-11770432 (Accessed: 12 September 2025).

[14] PYMNTS (2025) 'US senator raises alarm over Delta Air Line's testing of "personalized" pricing', *Pymnts.com*. Available at: www.pymnts.com/travel-payments/2025/us-senator-raises-alarm-over-delta-air-lines-testing-of-personalized-pricing/ (Accessed: 12 September 2025).

[15] Belanger, A. (2025) 'Delta denies using AI to come up with inflated, personalized prices', *Ars Technica*. Available at: https://arstechnica.com/tech-policy/2025/08/delta-denies-using-ai-to-come-up-with-inflated-personalized-prices/ (Accessed: 12 September 2025).

[16] Zschiegner, S. (2025) 'How grid edge computing is revolutionizing real-time power management', *POWER Magazine*. Available at: www.powermag.com/how-grid-edge-computing-is-revolutionizing-real-time-power-management/ (Accessed: 12 September 2025).

[17] Begumpeta, A. (no date) 'SWASTH-A-Healthcare-Chatbot: SWASTH is an AI-powered healthcare chatbot providing 24/7 medical assistance. It uses NLP and ML to analyse symptoms and predict illnesses. The chatbot then offers healthcare recommendations and medication suggestions. This project enhances healthcare accessibility and empowers individuals with basic medical advice'. Available at: https://github.com/Anjali-Begumpeta/SWASTH-A-Healthcare-Chatbot (Accessed: 18 October 2025).

[18] (No date) *Gavi.org*. Available at: www.gavi.org/vaccineswork/zimbabwe-ai-midwife-making-pregnancy-safer-underserved-women (Accessed: 12 September 2025).

[19] 'New report on IoT security underscores the current risk of unsecured devices and equipment' (2024) *IoT Business News*. Available at: https://iotbusinessnews.com/2024/02/15/01088-new-report-on-iot-security-underscores-the-current-risk-of-unsecured-devices-and-equipment/ (Accessed: 12 September 2025).

[20] As shared by a board director of the company, who requested anonymity.

[21] (No date) *Wsj.com*. Available at: www.wsj.com/articles/fraudsters-use-ai-to-mimic-ceos-voice-in-unusual-cybercrime-case-11567157402 (Accessed: 12 September 2025).

[22] Leng, C. and Ho-him, C. (2024) 'Arup lost $25mn in Hong Kong deepfake video conference scam', *Financial Times*, 16 May. Available at: www.ft.com/content/b977e8d4-664c-4ae4-8a8e-eb93bdf785ea (Accessed: 12 September 2025).

[23] Thomas, D. (2024) 'WPP boss targeted by deepfake scammers using voice clone', *Financial Times*, 10 May. Available at: www.ft.com/content/308c42af-2bf8-47e4-a360-517d5391b0b0 (Accessed: 12 September 2025).

[24] 'Denmark's groundbreaking move: Copyright for faces and voices' (2025) *Global Law Today*, 28 June. Available at: www.globallawtoday.com/law/legal-news/2025/06/denmarks-groundbreaking-move-copyright-for-faces-and-voices/ (Accessed: 12 September 2025).

[25] (No date) *Mit.edu*. Available at: https://sloanreview.mit.edu/article/how-ferrari-hit-the-brakes-on-a-deepfake-ceo/ (Accessed: 12 September 2025).

[26] Ch, S. (2025) *Swiss universities to release multilingual AI programme*, *www.swissinfo.ch*. Available at: www.swissinfo.ch/eng/swiss-ai/swiss-universities-to-releaselarge-language-model/89655364 (Accessed: 12 September 2025).

[27] 'Apertus: a fully open, transparent, multilingual language model' (no date) *ETH Zurich*. Available at: https://ethz.ch/en/news-and-events/eth-news/news/2025/09/press-release-apertus-a-fully-open-transparent-multilingual-language-model.html (Accessed: 12 September 2025).

[28] 'India's sovereign Large Language Model' (no date) *Sarvam.ai*. Available at: www.sarvam.ai/indias-sovereign-large-language-model (Accessed: 12 September 2025).

[29] Tech Desk (2025) '"India will make better SLM AI because…", says Infosys Chairman Nandan Nilekani; Here's why', *The Financial Express*, 31 August. Available at: www.financialexpress.com/life/technology-india-will-make-better-slm-ai-because-says-infosys-chairman-nandan-nilekani-heres-why-3962711/ (Accessed: 12 September 2025).

[30] *The Chosun Daily* (2025) 'South Korea to pour $735 bn into developing sovereign AI built on Korean language and data'. Available at: www.chosun.com/english/industry-en/2025/06/17/SRAB6HCZXJHM3NCJPZ3VALO6XU/ (Accessed: 12 September 2025).

[31] 'The AT Protocol' (no date) *Bsky.app*. Available at: https://docs.bsky.app/docs/advanced-guides/atproto (Accessed: 12 September 2025).

[32] Beckn Protocol specifications: Protocol-specifications: Core protocol specification for peer-to-peer consumer-provider interaction (no date). Available at: https://github.com/beckn/protocol-specifications (Accessed: 3 November 2025).

[33] Russon, M.-A. (2019) 'JP Morgan creates first US bank-backed crypto-currency', *BBC*, 14 February. Available at: www.bbc.co.uk/news/business-47240760 (Accessed: 12 September 2025).

[34] A stablecoin is pegged to a fiat currency such as the US dollar or Hong Kong dollar. Worldwide, stablecoin trading volume in 2024 reached US$27.6 trillion. It is debatable whether it is truly decentralized if it is pegged to fiat. For now stablecoins are another topic in the evolving technology and geopolitical landscape.

[35] Xue, Y. (2025) 'Standard Chartered, Animoca Brands, HKT to pursue Hong Kong dollar-backed stablecoin', *South China Morning Post*. Available at: www.scmp.com/business/article/3299034/standard-chartered-animoca-brands-hkt-pursue-hong-kong-dollar-backed-stablecoin (Accessed: 12 September 2025).

[36] Ryan, J. (2025) 'Tether holds an $8 billion pile of gold in a secret Swiss vault', *Bloomberg News*, 8 July. Available at: www.bloomberg.com/news/articles/2025-07-08/crypto-firm-tether-holds-8-billion-pile-of-gold-in-a-secret-swiss-vault (Accessed: 12 September 2025).

[37] Mason, E. (2025) 'Wyoming becomes the first to launch a state-issued stablecoin', *Bloomberg News*, 19 August. Available at: www.bloomberg.com/news/articles/2025-08-19/wyoming-becomes-the-first-to-launch-a-state-issued-stablecoin (Accessed: 12 September 2025).

[38] (No date) *Opendata.blog*. Available at: https://opendata.blog/open-data-initiatives-by-the-indian-government (Accessed: 12 September 2025).

[39] Warwick, M. (2025) 'Europe aims for digital independence with EuroStack', *TelecomTV*. Available at: www.telecomtv.com/content/digital-platforms-services/europe-aims-for-digital-independence-with-eurostack-52343/ (Accessed: 12 September 2025).

5 Business in choppy waters

[1] The Indigenous Affairs Team's Kirstie Wellauer and Boltje, S. (2025) 'Court finds no duty of care owed to Torres Strait Islanders over climate change', *ABC News*, 15 July. Available at: www.abc.net.au/news/2025-07-15/torres-strait-island-climate-case-court-decision/105532802 (Accessed: 12 September 2025).

[2] Buschschlüter, V. (2025) 'German court rejects Peruvian farmer's landmark climate case', *BBC*, 28 May. Available at: www.bbc.co.uk/news/articles/c5y5lwveqzno (Accessed: 12 September 2025).

[3] Zhang, T. (2020) 'Rest Super climate lawsuit has far-reaching implications', *Lawyers Weekly*. Available at: www.lawyersweekly.com.au/biglaw/29907-rest-super-climate-lawsuit-has-far-reaching-implications (Accessed: 12 September 2025).

[4] Frost, R. (2024) 'Historic European Court of Human Rights ruling backs Swiss women in climate change case', *Euronews*. Available at: www.euronews.com/green/2024/04/09/top-european-human-rights-court-could-rule-that-governments-have-to-protect-people-from-cl (Accessed: 12 September 2025).

[5] '"Their determination is heroic": Portuguese youth mount fresh climate lawsuit against government' (2025) *Euronews*. Available at: www.euronews.com/green/2025/04/09/their-determination-is-heroic-portuguese-youth-mount-fresh-climate-lawsuit-against-governm (Accessed: 12 September 2025).

[6] (No date). Available at: www.youtube.com/watch?v=67tHtpac5ws (Accessed for transcription on 26 June 2025).

[7] See www.mars.com/our-brands#Snacking (Accessed: 18 October 2025).

[8] 'Mars and Pairwise collaborate to accelerate cacao research and development' (2025) *Pairwise.com*, 6 August. Available at: www.pairwise.com/insights/mars-and-pairwise-collaborate-to-accelerate-cacao-research-and-development (Accessed: 14 September 2025).

[9] 'What is CRISPR? A bioengineer explains' (no date) *Stanford.edu*. Available at: https://news.stanford.edu/stories/2024/06/stanford-explainer-crispr-gene-editing-and-beyond (Accessed: 14 September 2025).

[10] Poynting, M. (2025) 'Three years left to limit warming to 1.5C, top scientists warn', *BBC*, 19 June. Available at: www.bbc.co.uk/news/articles/cn41927dj5zo (Accessed: 12 September 2025) citing Forster, P.M. et al. (2025) 'Indicators of Global Climate Change 2024: annual update of key indicators of the state of the climate system and human influence', *Earth System Science Data*, 17(6), 2641–80. Available at: https://doi.org/10.5194/essd-17-2641-2025.

[11] Bryan, K. (2024) 'Swiss Re says industry failed to estimate impact of extreme weather', *Financial Times*, 13 June. Available at: www.ft.com/content/48b3e54a-771a-4a12-a412-527c34311ca9 (Accessed: 12 September 2025).

[12] Read All News (2024) 'The African Risk Capacity white paper: Highlighting the increase in weather-related natural disasters in Africa', *Africa.com*. Available at: https://africa.com/the-african-risk-capacity-white-paper-highlighting-the-increase-in-weather-related-natural-disasters-in-africa/ (Accessed: 12 September 2025).

[13] Smith, I. (2024) 'Wanted: Country risk officers to tackle climate threat', *Financial Times*, 19 June. Available at: www.ft.com/content/f985e17f-5e6f-4dbc-94dd-4d0c03c56de8 (Accessed: 12 September 2025).
[14] (No date) *Reuters.com*. Available at: www.reuters.com/sustainability/how-insurance-innovation-could-unlock-billions-nature-based-climate-solutions-2025-01-13/ (Accessed: 12 September 2025).
[15] 'World risk poll 2024 report: Resilience in a changing world' (no date) *Lloyd's Register Foundation*. Available at: www.lrfoundation.org.uk/publications/resilience-in-a-changing-world? (Accessed: 12 September 2025).
[16] (No date) *Wsj.com*. Available at: www.wsj.com/articles/temperatures-are-higher-than-ever-but-companies-dont-want-to-talk-about-it-e5f30d5 (Accessed: 12 September 2025).
[17] (No date) *Wsj.com*. Available at: www.wsj.com/articles/global-banks-increase-fossil-fuel-funding-as-climate-pledges-crumble-9bbafce4 (Accessed: 12 September 2025).
[18] da Silva Bezerra, D. (2025) 'Nature-based solutions to climate change', *Scientific Reports*, 15, 22095. https://doi.org/10.1038/s41598-025-05678-7.
[19] Bhaduri, A. (2014) 'People of a semi-arid Rajasthan village battle Coca Cola', *India Water Portal*. Available at: www.indiawaterportal.org/drinking-water/people-semi-arid-rajasthan-village-battle-coca-cola (Accessed: 12 September 2025).
[20] *BBC* (no date) 'BBC - Press Office - Face the Facts investigates Coca-Cola plant'. Available at: www.bbc.co.uk/pressoffice/pressreleases/stories/2003/07_july/24/face_facts.shtml (Accessed: 12 September 2025).
[21] (No date) *Nytimes.com*. Available at: www.nytimes.com/2025/07/14/technology/meta-data-center-water.html (Accessed: 12 September 2025).
[22] Conversation with the leader in April 2025.
[23] (No date) *Edie.net*. Available at: www.edie.net/global-renewable-electricity-generation-surges-by-15-concentrated-in-asia/ (Accessed: 12 September 2025).
[24] Bloomberg News (2023) 'Singapore's MAS sets framework to improve transition financing', *Financial Post*. Available at: https://financialpost.com/pmn/business-pmn/singapores-mas-sets-framework-to-improve-transition-financing (Accessed: 14 September 2025).
[25] (No date) *Gov.sg*. Available at: www.edb.gov.sg/en/business-insights/insights/singapore-pledges-up-to-s669-million-to-finance-climate-action-in-asia.html (Accessed: 14 September 2025).
[26] ESG News (2024) 'Singapore joins EU and China in expanded green financing taxonomy', *ESG News*. Available at: https://esgnews.com/singapore-joins-eu-and-china-in-expanded-green-financing-taxonomy/ (Accessed: 14 September 2025).

[27] Peck, W.C. (2025) 'MAS, PBOC to deepen cooperation in green and transition finance', *The Business Times*. Available at: www.businesstimes.com.sg/companies-markets/mas-pboc-deepen-cooperation-green-and-transition-finance (Accessed: 14 September 2025).

[28] Mundy, S. (2025) 'Singapore's next strategic bet: green finance', *Financial Times*, 10 September. Available at: www.ft.com/content/c44dc366-29f0-4cc9-af4c-8ab99685c7b6 (Accessed: 14 September 2025).

[29] (No date) *Bloomberg.com*. Available at: www.bloomberg.com/news/newsletters/2025-09-03/blackrock-s-trans-atlantic-esg-dilemma (Accessed: 14 September 2025).

[30] (No date) *Bloomberg.com*. Available at: www.bloomberg.com/news/articles/2025-09-08/blackrock-explores-risk-models-to-add-scale-to-blended-finance (Accessed: 14 September 2025).

[31] Evans, A. (2017) *The myth gap: What happens when evidence and arguments aren't enough*. London: Eden Project Books.

[32] Armstrong, K. (2018) *A Short History of Myth*. Edinburgh: Canongate Canons.

[33] Jung, C.G. (1959) *Archetypes and the Collective Unconscious*. 2nd ed. Translated by R.F.C. Hull. London: Routledge.

[34] Didion, J. (2017) *The White Album*. London: Fourth Estate.

[35] 'Boards need to address barriers to climate change action' (no date) *Research Live*. Available at: www.research-live.com/article/news/boards_need_to_address_barriers_to_climate_change_action/id/5124693 (Accessed: 12 September 2025).

6 Geo-sensibilities and choices

[1] Fleary, S. (2025) 'Guyana is only country in the world that produces enough food to feed itself without imports', *Voice Online*. Available at: www.voice-online.co.uk/news/world-news/2025/06/25/guyana-is-only-country-in-the-world-that-produces-enough-food-to-feed-itself-without-imports/ (Accessed: 12 September 2025).

[2] Guyana (2020) *Norway's International Climate and Forest Initiative*. Available at: www.nicfi.no/partner-countries/guyana/ (Accessed: 14 September 2025).

[3] Bynoe, P., Wood, S. and Simmons, D. (2024) 'Greenhouse gas emissions from petroleum production in Guyana: An examination of the implications for the country's net carbon sink status', *Science Progress*, 107(1), 368504231218609. Available at: https://doi.org/10.1177/00368504231218609.

[4] Video on Dr Mohammed Irfaan Ali (no date). Available at: www.youtube.com/watch?v=5P4uAcGLWQg; BBC link, available at: www.bbc.co.uk/programmes/m001xt5x (Accessed: 18 October 2025).

[5] Excerpt (no date). Available at: www.bbc.co.uk/programmes/p0hrnsss (Accessed: 18 October 2025).

[6] Creemers, R., Webster, G. and Triolo, P. (2018) 'Translation: Cybersecurity Law of the People's Republic of China (effective June 1, 2017)', *DigiChina*. Available at: https://digichina.stanford.edu/work/translation-cybersecurity-law-of-the-peoples-republic-of-china-effective-june-1-2017/ (Accessed: 14 September 2025).

[7] 庞博 (no date) 关于印发《全国一体化大数据中心协同创新体系算力枢纽实施方案》的通知_国务院部门文件_中国政府网, *Gov.cn*. Available at: www.gov.cn/zhengce/zhengceku/2021-05/26/content_5612405.htm (Accessed: 14 September 2025).

[8] 'China's latest national infrastructure project spotlights computing capabilities' (2022) *Council on Foreign Relations*. Available at: www.cfr.org/blog/chinas-latest-national-infrastructure-project-spotlights-computing-capabilities (Accessed: 14 September 2025).

[9] Tong, Z. (2025) 'Why is China building AI centres on the roof of the world?', *South China Morning Post*. Available at: www.scmp.com/news/china/science/article/3316207/why-china-building-ai-centres-roof-world (Accessed: 14 September 2025).

[10] Hope, B. (2025) 'A spymaster sheikh controls a $1.5 trillion fortune. He wants to use it to dominate AI', *Wired*, 14 January. Available at: www.wired.com/story/uae-intelligence-chief-ai-money/ (Accessed: 12 September 2025).

[11] United Nations, Department of Economic and Social Affairs, Population Division (2024) *World Population Prospects 2024: Summary of Results.*

[12] Yinuo (2024) *Press release, United Nations Sustainable Development.* United Nations: Sustainable Development Goals. Available at: www.un.org/sustainable development/blog/2024/07/press-release-wpp2024/ (Accessed: 14 September 2025).

[13] The data and analysis in this and the following paragraph have been collated from a presentation by Professor Sarah Harper CBE, during PwC's programme for NEDs on 25 July 2025.

[14] Hennessee, J.P. et al. (2022) 'Relationship of prefrontal brain lateralization to optimal cognitive function differs with age', *NeuroImage*, 264, 119736. Available at: https://doi.org/10.1016/j.neuroimage.2022.119736.

[15] Strauch, B. (2011) *The secret life of the grown-up brain: Discover the surprising talents of the middle-aged mind.* Harlow: Penguin Books.

[16] Sax, L., Rachidi, A. and Anderson, S. (no date) 'Pro-natal policies work, but they come with a hefty price tag', *Institute for Family Studies*. Available at: https://ifstudies.org/blog/pro-natal-policies-work-but-they-come-with-a-hefty-price-tag (Accessed: 12 September 2025).
[17] Murphy, I. (2025) 'China's rare earth export controls', *Rare Earth Exchanges*. Available at: https://rareearthexchanges.com/news/chinas-rare-earth-export-controls-by-ian-murphy/ (Accessed: 12 September 2025).
[18] (No date) *Reuters.com*. Available at: www.reuters.com/world/china/chinas-rare-earth-export-controls-are-good-beijing-bad-business-2025-07-07/ (Accessed: 12 September 2025).
[19] White, E. and Liu, N. (2025) 'China's tighter export controls squeeze wider range of rare earths', *Financial Times*, 30 June. Available at: www.ft.com/content/13d18620-d3d8-417e-b7fb-40d97fc064bf (Accessed: 12 September 2025).
[20] White, E. and Liu, N. (2025) 'China's tighter export controls squeeze wider range of rare earths', *Financial Times*, 30 June. Available at: www.ft.com/content/13d18620-d3d8-417e-b7fb-40d97fc064bf (Accessed: 12 September 2025).
[21] Nnko, E. (2025) 'The alliance of Sahel states: The road towards nationalization', *Modern Diplomacy*. Available at: https://moderndiplomacy.eu/2025/05/04/the-alliance-of-sahel-states-the-road-towards-nationalization/ (Accessed: 14 September 2025).
[22] (No date) *Reuters.com*. Available at: www.reuters.com/world/africa/burkina-faso-completes-nationalisation-five-gold-mining-assets-2025-06-12/ (Accessed: 14 September 2025).
[23] Reuters (2025) 'DR Congo-Rwanda peace deal outlines US role in minerals sector', *South China Morning Post*. Available at: www.scmp.com/news/world/africa/article/3325486/dr-congo-rwanda-peace-deal-outlines-us-role-minerals-sector (Accessed: 14 September 2025).
[24] Chávez, S. and Muir, M. (2025) 'Pentagon strikes investment deal with US critical minerals producer', *Financial Times*, 10 July. Available at: www.ft.com/content/6693da6f-7cb7-4c74-8c4f-45b1bf533cbe (Accessed: 12 September 2025).
[25] Marks, S. (2025) 'The UAE in Africa: Power, influence and conflict', *Bloomberg News*, 8 July. Available at: www.bloomberg.com/news/features/2025-07-08/the-uae-in-africa-power-influence-and-conflict (Accessed: 14 September 2025).
[26] Asem, S. (2024) 'Egypt announces $35bn deal with UAE to buy premium Mediterranean area', *Middle East Eye*. Available at: www.middleeasteye.net/news/egypt-announces-massive-35-billion-deal-uae-develop-ras-el-hekma-north-coast (Accessed: 14 September 2025).

[27] 'DMCC future of trade report: Special critical minerals edition' (no date) *Futureoftrade.com*. Available at: www.futureoftrade.com/special-critical-minerals-edition-2025 (Accessed: 14 September 2025).

[28] (No date) *Reuters.com*. Available at: www.reuters.com/business/energy/indias-russian-oil-imports-rise-117-sept-aug-data-shows-2024-10-16/ (Accessed: 12 September 2025).

[29] Commonwealth and Development Office (2024) 'Economic ties with Southeast Asia strengthened as Foreign Secretary makes first visit to Indo-Pacific', *Gov.uk*. Available at: www.gov.uk/government/news/economic-ties-with-southeast-asia-strengthened-as-foreign-secretary-makes-first-visit-to-indo-pacific (Accessed: 14 September 2025).

[30] Cohen, M. and Iglesias, S. (2025) 'What is BRICS, the G-7 alternative being pushed by China?', *Bloomberg*. Available at: www.bloomberg.com/explainers/what-is-brics-who-s-in-what-do-they-want-and-why-it-matters (Accessed: 12 September 2025).

[31] Patrick, I. (2025) 'Brazil and China to study South American transcontinental railway project', *South China Morning Post*. Available at: www.scmp.com/news/china/diplomacy/article/3317462/brazil-and-china-study-south-american-transcontinental-railway-project (Accessed: 12 September 2025).

[32] 'Interview: China's tariff-free trade pact for African countries brings development opportunity, says Ghanaian analyst' (no date) *News.cn*. Available at: https://english.news.cn/20250627/d6bd6d3d2bdb464d9c55dc268e4267bb/c.html (Accessed: 12 September 2025).

[33] Addamah, S. (no date) 'India and Ghana cement strategic ties with landmark agreements during Modi's historic visit', *Medafricatimes.com*. Available at: https://medafricatimes.com/41100-india-and-ghana-cement-strategic-ties-with-landmark-agreements-during-modis-historic-visit.html (Accessed: 14 September 2025).

[34] (No date) *Modernghana.com*. Available at: www.modernghana.com/news/1414453/china-ghana-mark-65-years-of-diplomatic-ties-with.html (Accessed: 14 September 2025).

[35] *MSN* (no date) *Msn.com*. Available at: www.msn.com/en-in/news/other/modi-makes-diplomatic-push-in-africa-says-continent-must-not-be-just-a-source-for-raw-materials/ar-AA1Ikn2r? (Accessed: 12 September 2025).

[36] Cotterill, J., Daniels, J. and Murray, C. (2025) 'Developing countries swap out of dollar debt to cut borrowing costs', *Financial Times*, 2 September. Available at: www.ft.com/content/36f82232-d970-405c-97f6-8ce98725684b (Accessed: 14 September 2025).

[37] Chia, O. (2025) 'How oil has brought China, Russia and India closer together', *BBC*, 2 September. Available at: www.bbc.co.uk/news/articles/c627p49lp40o (Accessed: 14 September 2025).

[38] 'NATO defense spending tracker' (2025) *Atlantic Council*. Available at: www.atlanticcouncil.org/commentary/trackers-and-data-visualizations/nato-defense-spending-tracker/ (Accessed: 12 September 2025).

[39] (No date) *Reuters.com*. Available at: www.reuters.com/business/aerospace-defense/bae-ceo-esg-investors-less-frosty-defence-sector-since-ukraine-war-2023-08-02/ (Accessed: 12 September 2025).

[40] European defence holding company, resulting from the merger of Krauss Maffei Wegmann Nexter Defense Systems.

[41] *Reuters* (2024) 'How drone combat in Ukraine is changing warfare', 26 March. Available at: www.reuters.com/graphics/UKRAINE-CRISIS/DRONES/dwpkeyjwkpm/ (Accessed: 12 September 2025).

[42] Razzouk, N., Seputyte, M. and Wass, S. (2025) 'Europe's citizen soldiers', *Bloomberg*. Available at: www.bloomberg.com/features/2025-europe-russia-army-conscription/ (Accessed: 12 September 2025).

[43] Suárez, J. and Hannikainen, I.R. (2025) 'Integration gaps persist despite immigrants' value assimilation: evidence from the European Social Survey', *Frontiers in Sociology*, 10, 1504127. Available at: https://doi.org/10.3389/fsoc.2025.1504127.

[44] 'Overview of data sovereignty laws by country' (2024) *InCountry*, 9 April. Available at: https://incountry.com/blog/overview-of-data-sovereignty-laws-by-country/ (Accessed: 12 September 2025).

[45] 'According to a recent study, the majority of companies see data sovereignty as a strategic imperative point' (2025) *A1 Digital*. Available at: www.a1.digital/press/majority-of-companies-see-data-sovereignty-as-a-strategic-imperative-point/ (Accessed: 12 September 2025).

[46] Farooquee, N. (2025) 'Prada: Luxury label acknowledges Indian roots of footwear design after backlash', *BBC*, 30 June. Available at: www.bbc.co.uk/news/articles/cj4e24n20wwo (Accessed: 12 September 2025).

[47] Tex, B. (2025) 'Prime minister shri Narendra Modi addresses the Bharat Tex 2025', *Bharat Tex*, 16 February. Available at: www.bharat-tex.com/prime-minister-shri-narendra-modi-addresses-the-bharat-tex-2025/ (Accessed: 12 September 2025).

[48] 'The coffee war: Ethiopia and the Starbucks story' (no date) *ip-advantage*. Available at: www.wipo.int/en/web/ip-advantage/w/stories/the-coffee-war-ethiopia-and-the-starbucks-story (Accessed: 12 September 2025).

[49] 'From exploitation to empowerment: The Maasai tribe's journey to intellectual property ownership' (no date) *Center for International and Security Studies at Maryland.* Available at: https://cissm.umd.edu/news/exploitation-empowerment-maasai-tribes-journey-intellectual-property-ownership (Accessed: 12 September 2025).

[50] BBC News (2021) 'Rio Tinto chief to step down over cave destruction', *BBC*, 3 March. Available at: www.bbc.co.uk/news/business-56261514 (Accessed: 12 September 2025).

[51] Hume, N. and Mooney, A. (2020) 'Rio Tinto investors demand action after Aboriginal cave destruction', *Financial Times*, 21 June. Available at: www.ft.com/content/6db79b46-8e46-4e89-8688-97064effbc61 (Accessed: 12 September 2025).

[52] Correspondence with Zoho Corporation in July 2025.

[53] Mohan, M. (2025) 'Zoho's business model: How does zoho earn money?', *The Business Scroll.* Available at: www.thebusinessscroll.com/zohos-business-model/ (Accessed: 12 September 2025).

[54] Thomas, D. (2025) 'How can African brands win customers back from western giants?', *African Business*. Available at: https://african.business/2025/06/trade-investment/how-can-african-brands-win-customers-back-from-western-giants (Accessed: 12 September 2025).

[55] Godbold, N. (2025) 'Which Central Banks bought and sold the most gold in 2024?', *Luxurious Magazine*. Available at: www.luxuriousmagazine.com/central-bank-gold-buying-selling-2024/ (Accessed: 12 September 2025).

[56] 'Banking on gold: 15 years of central bank gold buying' (no date) *Auronum.co.uk*. Available at: https://auronum.co.uk/banking-on-gold-15-years-of-central-bank-gold-buying/ (Accessed: 12 September 2025).

7 How it's going...

[1] Batista, C. et al. (2025) 'Brain drain or brain gain? Effects of high-skilled international emigration on origin countries', *Science*, 388(6749), eadr8861. Available at: https://doi.org/10.1126/science.adr8861.

[2] Bender, E.M. et al. (2021) 'On the dangers of stochastic parrots: Can language models be too big? 🦜', in *Proceedings of the 2021 ACM Conference on Fairness, Accountability, and Transparency*. New York: ACM. Available at: https://dl.acm.org/doi/10.1145/3442188.3445922.

[3] (No date) Available at: https://x.com/elonmusk/status/1936333964693885089 (Accessed: 18 October 2025).

[4] Durand, C. and Milberg, W. (2019). 'Intellectual monopoly in global value chains', *Review of International Political Economy*, 27, 1–26. Available at: https://doi.org/10.1080/09692290.2019.1660703.

[5] Heaven, W.D. (2025) 'What comes next for AI copyright lawsuits?', *Technology Review*, 1 July. Available at: www.technologyreview.com/2025/07/01/1119486/ai-copyright-meta-anthropic/ (Accessed: 12 September 2025).

[6] Belanger, A. (2025) '"First of its kind" AI settlement: Anthropic to pay authors $1.5 billion', *Ars Technica*. Available at: https://arstechnica.com/tech-policy/2025/09/first-of-its-kind-ai-settlement-anthropic-to-pay-authors-1-5-billion/ (Accessed: 14 September 2025).

[7] Belanger, A. (2025b) 'Judge: Anthropic's $1.5B settlement is being shoved "down the throat of authors,"' *Ars Technica*. Available at: https://arstechnica.com/tech-policy/2025/09/judge-anthropics-1-5b-settlement-is-being-shoved-down-the-throat-of-authors/ (Accessed: 14 September 2025).

[8] Bauman, B. (2025) 'A.I., copyright and the case that could shape creative ownership standards', *Observer*, 10 July. Available at: https://observer.com/2025/07/midjourney-disney-nbc-lawsuit-generative-ai-copyright/ (Accessed: 12 September 2025).

[9] Zwiezen, Z. (2025) 'Warner bros. sues midjourney over turning batman, joker, and more into AI slop', *Kotaku*. Available at: https://kotaku.com/wb-lawsuit-midjourney-ai-art-slop-batman-joker-disney-nbc-2000623232 (Accessed: 14 September 2025).

[10] *Mumbai Indians* (no date) *Mumbai Indians*. Available at: www.mumbaiindians.com/players (Accessed: 12 September 2025).

[11] (No date) *Metr.org*. Available at: https://metr.org/Early_2025_AI_Experienced_OS_Devs_Study.pdf (Accessed: 12 September 2025).

[12] Rockerbie, D. W., & Easton, S. T. (2022). 'Race to the podium: Separating and conjoining the car and driver in F1 racing', *Applied Economics*, 54(54), 6272–85. Available at: https://doi.org/10.1080/00036846.2022.2083068.

[13] *WIRED Summer Lab* (no date) *Wirededucation.com*. Available at: www.wirededucation.com/ (Accessed: 12 September 2025).

[14] Chataut, R. (2024) 'Undersea cables are the unseen backbone of the global internet', *The Conversation*. Edited by E. Smalley. Available at: https://doi.org/10.64628/aai.f4kqfj499.

[15] Asadu, C. (2024) *Internet Outage Hits Several African Countries as Undersea Cables Fail*, *AP News*. Available at: https://apnews.com/article/africa-internet-outage-undersea-cables-failure-ac67fd11b4d9ae7cb3959622c5e9e78b (Accessed: 12 September 2025).

[16] (No date) *Wsj.com*. Available at: www.wsj.com/world/europe/sweden-says-second-undersea-cable-damaged-in-baltic-sea-d9f21fea (Accessed: 12 September 2025).

[17] *GMES and Africa Programme Now the African Space Agency as Continental Flagship Initiative* (no date) *Csir.co.za*. Available at: www.csir.co.za/gmes-and-africa-programme-now-african-space-agency-continental-flagship-initiative (Accessed: 12 September 2025).

[18] Mthembu, T. (2025) *SA's Youth Unemployment Crisis can Become an Opportunity*, *The Citizen*. Available at: www.citizen.co.za/news/opinion/sas-youth-unemployment-crisis-can-become-an-opportunity/ (Accessed: 12 September 2025).

[19] *MSN* (no date) *Msn.com*. Available at: www.msn.com/en-in/money/topstories/joblessness-steady-at-56-in-june-youth-jobless-rate-still-above-15/ar-AA1IG7CU (Accessed: 12 September 2025).

[20] *Financial Times* (2025) 'It's a bad time to be a graduate', 6 July. Available at: www.ft.com/content/002a0943-f977-44bd-bc78-957c877dfed1 (Accessed: 12 September 2025).

[21] *Harvard Business Review* (2025) 'How ageism is undermining AI implementation', 25 February. Available at: https://hbr.org/2025/02/how-ageism-is-undermining-ai-implementation (Accessed: 12 September 2025).

[22] (No date). Available at: https://x.com/MPSomerstein/status/1659203829026680838 (Accessed: 18 October 2025).

[23] (No date). Available at: https://x.com/AuthorJMac/status/1773679197631701238 (Accessed: 18 October 2025).

[24] In the HEIT story shared on page 80, the reader may note that the board had access to the data platform that tracked the performance of our operational assets in various different revenue streams and markets.

[25] Edward N. Luttwak defines geoeconomics as 'the admixture of the logic of conflict with the methods of commerce'. From *Geopolitics to Geo-Economics: Logic of Conflict, Grammar of Commerce* (no date). Edward N. Luttwak. *The National Interest*, 20 (Summer 1990), 17–23. Available at: www.jstor.org/stable/42894676?seq=1

[26] (No date) *Eetimes.eu*. Available at: www.eetimes.eu/risc-v-to-move-hq-to-switzerland-amid-trade-war-concerns/ (Accessed: 12 September 2025).

[27] BBC News (2021) 'James Dyson says Brexit has given him "freedom,"' *BBC*, 14 April. Available at: www.bbc.co.uk/news/business-56741000 (Accessed: 12 September 2025).

[28] *MSN* (no date) *Msn.com*. Available at: www.msn.com/en-gb/cars/news/lotus-isnt-closing-its-uk-base-but-is-exploring-options-to-stay-competitive/ar-AA1HHNr0 (Accessed: 12 September 2025).

[29] Blackwell, C. (2025) 'Proton relocates to Germany, Norway over Swiss surveillance laws', *WebProNews*. Available at: www.webpronews.com/proton-relocates-to-germany-norway-over-swiss-surveillance-laws/ (Accessed: 12 September 2025).

[30] Herrera, R. (2025) 'The Impact of GLP 1 drugs on the Food Industry', *UC Davis Innovation Institute for Food and Health*. Available at: https://foodandhealth.ucdavis.edu/the-impact-of-glp-1-drugs-on-the-food-industry-foodtech-11-doon-insights/ (Accessed: 12 September 2025).

[31] 'Un nouveau rapport révèle que le Royaume-Uni et les États-Unis voient toujours l'Afrique sous l'angle de la pauvreté, de la corruption et de la nature – mais il existe une solution – Africa No Filter' (no date) *Africanofilter.org*. Available at: https://africanofilter.org/stereotypes-about-africa-us-uk-french (Accessed: 12 September 2025).

[32] Brand, R. (2025) 'African Union backs campaign to adopt more realistic world map', *Bloomberg News*, 19 August. Available at: www.bloomberg.com/news/articles/2025-08-19/african-union-back-campaign-to-adopt-more-realistic-world-map (Accessed: 12 September 2025).

Resources

Uncharted Spaces community

www.unchartedspaces.info/

Books

1. *Board Talk: 18 Crucial Conversations that Count Inside and Outside the Boardroom* by Kathryn Bishop & Gillian Camm; Practical Inspiration Publishing, 2023

2. *The Art and Psychology of Board Relationships: The Secret Life of Boards* by Joy Harcup & Helen Hopper; Routledge, 2023

3. *Boards: A Practical Perspective* by Patrick Dunne (2nd edition); Governance Publishing & Information Services Ltd, 2021

4. *How Boards Work: And How They Can Work Better in a Chaotic World* by Dambisa Moyo; The Bridge St Press, 2021

5. *On Board: The Insider's Guide to Surviving Life In The Boardroom* by Sir John Tusa; Bloomsbury, 2021

6. *Boards That Deliver – Advancing Corporate Governance from Compliance to Competitive Advantage* by Ram Charan; Jossey Bass, 2005

7. *The Great Chair: A Window on Effective Board Leadership* by Brian Hayward; Friesen Press, 2020

8. *The Fish Rots from the Head* by Bob Garrett; Profile Books, 2010

Board Directors' networks and communities

- Pan-Africa:
  - African Corporate Governance Network (https://afcgn.com/)
  - The Boardroom Africa (https://theboardroomafrica.com/)
- Emerging Markets:
  - Impact Boards Emerging Markets (www.iboardsem.com/)
- Global:
  - InfraNEDs (women NEDs on real assets boards) (www.infraneds.org/)
  - Critical Eye (https://criticaleye.com/inspiring/welcome.cfm)
- UK:
  - WB Directors (https://wbdirectors.co.uk/)
  - Empowering People of Colour (www.epocnetwork.com/)
  - Nurole (www.nurole.com/)
  - NED on Board (www.nedonboard.com/)
  - NEDs in Financial Services (https://nedsinfs.com/)
- Europe:
  - European Women on Boards (https://europeanwomenonboards.eu/)
  - Professional Boards Forum (www.boardsforum.co.uk/)
- Switzerland:
  - The Boardroom (www.the-boardroom.ch)
- India:
  - Institute of Directors India (www.iodglobal.com/)
- Singapore:
  - Singapore Institute of Directors (www.sid.org.sg/)
- Hong Kong and China:
  - Hong Kong Institute of Directors (www.hkiod.com/)
- Australia:
  - Women on Boards Australia (www.womenonboards.net/)
  - Future Directors (www.futuredirectors.com/home)

- USA:
  - Black Women on Boards (www.bwob.io/)
  - Illumyn Impact (www.illumynimpact.org/about-us)
  - 50-50 Women on Boards (https://5050wob.com/)
  - Women Corporate Directors (https://wcdglobal.org/)
  - National Association of Corporate Directors (www.nacdonline.org/)
  - Private Directors Association (www.privatedirectors.org/)
  - Latino Corporate Directors Association (https://latinocorporatedirectors.org/)
  - Association of LGBTQ+ Corporate Directors (https://lgbtqdirectors.org/)
  - Ascend Pinnacle for Pan-Asian Board Directors (www.ascendleadership.org/pinnacle)

Acknowledgements

Without the generosity of the many board directors, Chairs, CEOs and board advisers who agreed to be interviewed and then contributed their experiences and opinions candidly, this book would have been an exercise in solipsism. I owe special thanks to Kumeshnee West of The Boardroom Africa for catalyzing introductions to board directors in many corporations in several African nations. I also hat-tip friends, colleagues, and members of my family in many countries around the world with whom I have had hundreds of conversations over the years about their experiences around the themes in this book. I am grateful to each one of them and I respect that many did not wish to be named here.

Those who kindly agreed to be named are: Adam Saunders, Angela Gichaga, Ashwin West, Bart Shuldman, Carrie Freeman, Catriona Schmolke CBE FREng, Charity Chanda Lumpa, Charles Wright, Davina Walter, Devyani Vaishampayan, Eshna Gogia, Fiona Hathorn, Hounaïda Lasry, Dr Hugh McNeal, Sir Ivan Rogers, Janine Freeman, Joanna Bonnett, Karina Litvack, Karl Schaecke, Makarand Sahasrabuddhe, Mark Wood, Mary Curnock Cook CBE, Namrata Rana, Norman Crighton, Ndidi Okonkwo Nwuneli, Nicola Zotta, Paul Viner, Rajeev Sawhney, Professor Rama Bijapurkar, Santosh Pillai, Shalini Bhateja, Tauqeer Jamadar, Ved Sen, Vrushali Gaud, Urmi Dutta Roy, and William Rickett CB.

For answering my very specific questions, I owe huge thanks to Karina Luchinkina, Nanya Srivastava, Praval Singh, Rajeshwari (Rajee) Krishnamurthy, and Simon Harris.

For sharing insights and experiences generously through the years either at events or in conversations, I owe gratitude to many and some of their names, where the events were public or where they agreed to be quoted, appear peppered throughout the text.

For letting me share the Harmony Energy Income Trust story arc, I am grateful to my board Chair Norman Crighton, and my board colleagues William Rickett CB, Janine Freeman, and Dr Hugh McNeal. Thanks are also due to Peter Kavanagh and the Harmony team, and our advisers.

For getting me started on my boards journey, and for being my coach and mentor during my Board Apprenticeship, all my gratitude is due to Davina Walter, without whom there may not have been a book at all.

For reading early drafts and for providing critical comments, I am grateful to Joanna Bonnett, Steve Landes, Syamant Sandhir, and Alan Patrick.

For handholding me through the entire process of publishing, I cannot be more thankful to the Practical Inspiration Publishing team. Alison Jones has created something very special in the publishing world and when she says she leads with author care, she lives and breathes it.

For moral support, cheerleading, food, and warm cookies as I was writing, I am eternally grateful to Katie Harris, Lizzie Harris, Meeta Sengupta, Madhvi Kshatriya, my sister Gunjan Yogendra, Kavita Agarwal, Asit Gupta, Steve Landes, and Syamant Sandhir; they tolerated meltdowns and demands for conversations, and were there when I needed them to be available.

The acknowledgements would be incomplete without a mention of Robert A.G. Monks and his transformational work in stakeholder capitalism and shareholder activism. He passed away in 2025 at 91, just as I was beginning to write this book.

For setting a challenge in January 2015 to write a book, I nod to my old buddy Kannan Ramachandran, who has had to wait over a decade for it. For winning the challenge years ahead and for delightful and thought-provoking conversations always, I hat-tip my old friend Ved Sen, and strongly recommend his 2022 book *Doing Digital: The Guide to Digital for Non-Technical Leaders.*

For never letting me imagine something was beyond me, I will always be grateful to my late father. For showing me it was possible to be an engineer by training but a polymath by choice, I will always be grateful to my dearest late older cousin. For never seeking to dim my light and instead for supporting me while I paved my yellow brick road, and for sharing insights and experiences of boardroom dynamics, some of which are in this book, I will always be grateful to my late husband. This book is for all three of you.

I wrote this book in the 50th year of my mother's death and I hope she will have approved.

All errors of omission or commission are mine alone.

Index

A quick word from Practical Inspiration Publishing...

We hope you found this book both practical and inspiring – that's what we aim for with every book we publish.

We publish titles on topics ranging from leadership, entrepreneurship, HR and marketing to self-development and wellbeing.

Find details of all our books at: www.practicalinspiration.com

Did you know...

We can offer discounts on bulk sales of all our titles – ideal if you want to use them for training purposes, corporate giveaways or simply because you feel these ideas deserve to be shared with your network.

We can even produce bespoke versions of our books, for example with your organization's logo and/or a tailored foreword.

To discuss further, contact us on info@practicalinspiration.com.

Got an idea for a business book?

We may be able to help. Find out about more about publishing in partnership with us at: bit.ly/PIpublishing.

Follow us on social media...

 @PIPTalking

 @pip_talking

 @practicalinspiration

 @piptalking

 Practical Inspiration Publishing

www.ingramcontent.com/pod-product-compliance
Lightning Source LLC
Chambersburg PA
CBHW021925190326
41519CB00009B/916